The Hidden Edge of Exmoor

First published in 2011 by Thematic Trails
7 Norwood Avenue, Kingston Bagpuize with Southmoor
Oxfordshire OX13 5AD   www.thematic-trails.org

ISBN 978-0-948444-57-9
© David Kester Webb and Elizabeth Webb 2011
Printed by Information Press, Eynsham, Oxfordshire. UK

All photography and paintings in this book are by David Kester Webb, unless otherwise stated.
Primary editing was by Elizabeth Webb. Final proof editor, Janet Keene.
Design and lay-out by Peter Keene.

Information for the reader

Within this book there unfolds a fascinating history of the exploration of the cliffs of the Exmoor coast. It should have a wide appeal for anyone interested in the landscape of this often hidden coastline, if only to be enchanted by the way Kester Webb has captured the, often fleeting and intangible, beauty of the cliffs. This he has done with a remarkable set of photographs and paintings, supported by vivid descriptions of his experiences, born of a long period of exploration.

The continuous unifying element running through the book is the development of the 'Exmoor Traverse' which involves a series of cliff 'climbs' and scrabbles connecting the sea cliffs of this coast from east to west. Kester is at pains to stress that this book is not written as a climber's guide and should never be treated as such. However, it does allow readers the pleasure of climbing these cliffs, even if only in their imagination.

Titles of Publications: Publications mentioned in the text and written in italics. Main literary sources are listed in a bibliography on page 119.
Glossary: Some more unusual terms are explained in a glossary on page 120 and are printed in *italics* the first time they are mentioned in the text.
Quotes: are enclosed with single inverted commas and sometimes enclosed within a coloured panel.
Stream numbering: Coastal streams or waterfalls mentioned by name are often also listed by the numbering system used by Newell Arber, as originally shown by a map, facing page 165, in *'The Coast Scenery of North Devon'*.
Altitude in feet: Because so many of the maps and recorded statements refer to pre-decimal days, all heights are normally given in feet unless directly quoting metres.

Cover photo: Picnic on Cormorant Rock; framed by the Valley of Rocks, Lynton.
Frontispiece: The 'A' Cave bridge, supporting Dave Taylor, Terry Cheek and Martin Webb.
Contents page photos: Left: Elizabeth Webb climbing.
                    Right: Climbing Wringapeak; Terry Cheek and Martin Webb.

The Hidden Edge
of Exmoor

Photography and Paintings by
David Kester Webb

Edited by Elizabeth F. Webb

FOREWORD
by
MURIEL AGNES ARBER

Much water has flowed to sea out of Sherracombe since my father, E. A. Newell Arber, carrying a stand camera and glass plates, landed from a boat to take a time-exposure photograph of the waterfall. Kester Webb's achievement in making a complete traverse of the Exmoor cliffs would have given him profound satisfaction. This book is the record of that exploration, illustrated with photographs, some of which show places that no one has ever seen before.

Muriel on the Exmoor coast with the Webb family: Martin, Liz, Muriel, Rebekah.

David Kester Webb
who has become the "whoever"
of the last line of page 26.

Muriel A. Arber
30 August 1997

ACKNOWLEDGEMENTS

We owe an enormous debt of gratitude to our dear friend, the late Muriel Arber and to everyone who has been involved in our *Hidden Edge of Exmoor* exploration.

Especially we thank our mentors and publishers, Peter and Janet Keene, without whom this fifty year project would not have materialised as a finished book; our generous friends and sponsors Mollie Rodber, Trish Isherwood, David Hillebrandt, Tim and Jeanne Webb and those who have so kindly subscribed.

Our most grateful thanks go to our geological mentors, Eric Robinson and Chris Wood, for their invaluable advice and guidance; to our intrepid aircraft pilots, Richard Webber, Nigel Skinner and David Berger, for their interest and skill; to Brian Williams, Harriet Bridle and the late Michael Ireland, for their helpful advice and support; and to our painstaking proof readers, Sue Lane and Jeanne Webb.

We are so fortunate to have enjoyed the good company and trust of all those explorers who have dared to join in our expeditions. For sharing their knowledge and their exceptional climbing skills, two amongst them deserve especial thanks, the late Cyril Manning and the indomitable Terry Cheek.

Lastly we thank our offspring, Rebekah and Martin, for their resilience.

Falcons on the Exmoor cliffs

CONTENTS

page

INTRODUCTION AND HISTORICAL BACKGROUND

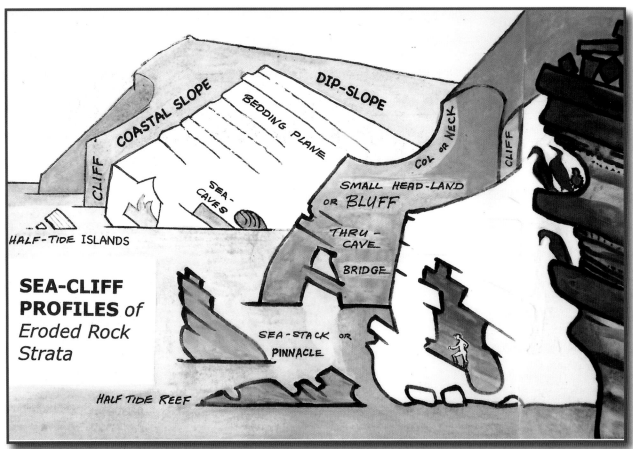

SEA-CLIFF PROFILES of Eroded Rock Strata

COASTAL SLOPE — CLIFF — BEDDING PLANE — DIP-SLOPE — COL OR NECK — CLIFF — SMALL HEAD-LAND OR BLUFF — SEA-CAVES — THRU-CAVE — BRIDGE — HALF-TIDE ISLANDS — SEA-STACK OR PINNACLE — HALF TIDE REEF

While over a thousand people may have climbed Mount Everest and many thousands may have walked England's South West Coast Path, very few have traversed the whole of the Exmoor Coast down at sea level, along what we have called *The Hidden Edge of Exmoor.* The Exmoor Traverse is a serious mountaineering venture that is compounded by a tide that can rise vertically at six feet an hour and by cliffs that tower over six hundred feet in places. Out of sight of civilisation it is an awe-inspiring wilderness, boasting the highest marine cliff in England, a waterfall as high as Niagara and a colony of ancient stunted yew trees that may prove to be the largest in Britain.

In an age when we have grown accustomed to elaborate expeditions to the ends of the earth, the story of the First Traverse of the Exmoor Coast, above 'The Severn Sea', reads like an adventure of the nineteenth century. That it was achieved in the mid-twentieth century and completed by so few people, indicates just how wild and remote is this part of the world.

This coast has always been regarded as hostile, inaccessible and dangerous; suitable only for smugglers and brigands, and used reluctantly only by trading boatmen from South Wales. The north-facing shore is mostly in shade, damp and uninviting; even the satellite photographs show little more than the black shadow of the cliffs from Woody Bay to Combe Martin.

No doubt the local inhabitants have in the past scrambled up sea-cliffs to collect birds' eggs and fat fledglings for the cooking pot. Boat-builders at one time harvested the curved wind-combed oak trees that grow out and up from the vertical cliffs, and longbow archers of Old England would have harvested the abundant yew trees below Martinhoe. It is known too that slaves were sent up cliffs to collect rare lichen to make royal purple dye.

In the 19th century, the dramatic scenery attracted landscape painters and lithographers, such as J.M. Turner, Samuel Palmer and George Rowe. From the 1830s onward, poets like Percy Bysshe

Shelley and Samuel T. Coleridge visited and were inspired by Exmoor's romantic beauty. Charles Kingsley, as a young curate, also frequented the area and the grandson of a Rector of Combe Martin, one R.D. Blackmore, used his local knowledge in writing *Lorna Doone.*

Victorian culture generated a wide interest in botany and geology, motivating explorers like the Bishop James Hannington to pioneer paths 'down-over' the sea-cliffs when he was a young curate in the 1870s. Preventative Officers of the Revenue established a path traversing the coastal slopes from Minehead to Combe Martin, when, according to the local Sector Coastguard 'revenue evasion made smuggling an attractive proposition, even on this dangerous coast but even then patrols could not fully observe the vertical sea-cliffs and the beaches below.

Palæobotanist, E.A. Newell Arber, noted the problem in 1908, when researching the seaward face of the curving *hog's-back cliffs*, as he termed them. He observed that there were only a few places where high cliff-faces could be inspected from the path: notably where the shoreline faces north-west, i.e. the Foreland (viewed from Lynton) and also the massive Highcliff of Ramsay Head (viewed from the Holdstone Path). Wringapeak Headland can be seen from the corner of the path through Hollow Combe, but England's highest sea-cliff, Great Hangman Gut, shows only its very top to those who venture around Great Hangman on the old Miners' Track.

The Coast Path rises to the 820 ft contour in places and huge gullies or *guts* slice into the cliffs. Anyone exploring below the path soon discovers that the area of coastal slope is much larger than it looks on the map.

The Pioneers of the 1960s, planning to explore the fifteen miles of indented shore-line from Lynmouth to Combe Martin, had first to conduct a serious survey of the cliffs, their aim being to establish safe routes to and from the beach below. They trudged up and down huge expanses of 45° slopes, often fighting through wet, hostile vegetation of briars and gorse. These *recces* involved carrying heavy equipment: ice-axes, lump hammers, three-foot long iron stakes, coils of rope, bow-saws, loppers, secateurs and reap-hooks. Down at sea level, the ubiquitous slippery seaweed was an ever-present hazard for beach crawlers.

The northern boundary of the Exmoor National Park is twenty-five miles in length and most of the shoreline can be walked at low tide. There are precious few stretches of sand, for the beach is mostly boulders ranging in size from footballs to fridges and from cars to vans. Beaches that are parallel to the tidal currents tend to be narrow and steeper than where the beach faces north-west.

Where the boulders peter out explorers are forced onto ledges, *reefs* and *bedrock* at the foot of the cliff. Ledges often lead to vertical walls that drop straight down into the sea even on the lowest of tides. At these points the explorer has to become a rock climber. The original pioneers often found themselves in remote mountainous terrain with the biggest hazard, as always, the sea. Tidal currents can flow around headlands at swift walking pace and the sea-state can change suddenly, with big waves arriving unannounced. Most important of all, the Bristol Channel tidal range, one of the highest in the world, can rise thirty feet in six hours.

Since 1960, the Exmoor Coast Traverse to our knowledge, has been completed by only **twenty** explorers. All were experienced mountaineers and at least medium-grade rock-climbers. Travelling as a team, always a minimum of three, we were familiar with the weather forecast, the tidal predictions and the location of escape routes.

We had to be self-supporting and capable of self-rescue. The rule was to keep dry-shod within the littoral zone (i.e. between high and low water mark) and to not go into the sea, except in an emergency and then only on a *belay*ed rope. The Ilfracombe Coastguard Sector Officer was always informed of our plans, and occasionally joined us.

It was E.A. Newell Arber, of Cambridge, who was the inspiration for our Exmoor Traverse Adventure. In his book *The Coast Scenery of North Devon,* 1911, he writes how surprised he was to find 'how little this coast had been explored, from the point of view of its geology and scenery' and how astonished to find 'how interesting the coast really is'. He found himself 'being led away from fossil botany to explore its undescribed wonders'.

In many respects, with regard to the awe inspired by the place, nothing has changed in the last hundred years. Newell Arber maintained it would require a serious mountaineering expedition to explore the sea-cliffs thoroughly:-

'It would be a proud accomplishment to have traversed the whole of the shoreline from Porlock (westwards). Whoever manages to accomplish this feat in the future will have seen wonders in the way of cliff scenery and can boast a remarkable record, similar to climbing an un-trodden Alpine peak.'   [*The Coast Scenery of North Devon* by E.A. Newell Arber, 1911. Page 26.]

The story of *The Hidden Edge of Exmoor* is our response to Arber's Challenge of a 100 years ago.

Newell Arber in 1908

EARLY PIONEERS

A. JAMES HANNINGTON 1847-1885

James Hannington's 1870 Diary is the earliest known record of a climber on the Exmoor sea-cliffs and the 1888 Ordnance Survey Map of Martinhoe show two tracks marked 'Hannington's Path'.

Hannington was born at Hurstpierpoint, Sussex in 1847. He entered St. Mary's Hall, Oxford, in 1868 to study theology, with a view to ordination. His Principal disapproved of his lack of progress and in 1870, aged 23, he was sent to Martinhoe Rectory, 'a lonely place and out of the way', to study for his B.A. under the supervision of the Rector, the Revd. Charles Scriven. He was ordained in 1874, aged 27, and took charge of the small parish of Trentishoe, as well as serving at Martinhoe.

According to E. C. Dawson's biography, *James Hannington. A History of His Life and Work. 1847-1885*, the Principal could not have known that 'this perplexing undergraduate would find in Devonshire peasant folk and still more in Devonshire cliffs and sea, distractions even greater than college life could offer him'.

He was immediately captivated by the cliffs of Martinhoe and Trentishoe and took to exploring them on his pony; when he was not riding across the treacherous Moor to take services at scattered parishes, some as far away as Challacombe. Hannington was soon looking for ways down the cliffs, or cleves as the locals called them, perilously scrambling from ledge to ledge to search for plants and for chough's eggs to eat.
On one occasion he spied the western portal of a large sea-cave, four hundred feet below. Anxious to investigate, he and 'young Scriven', the Rector's eighteen-year-old son, George, scrambled down the cliffs above the 'vasty deep' to discover what they called Cave Scriven. Hannington decided it must be seen by the whole Rectory family and that a path must be engineered for the purpose. He hired two 'able-bodied' labourers, an old crippled cragsman called Richard Jones, and enlisted the help of Rectory servants and various parishioners.

According to his diary on Sept. 1st. 1870, they armed themselves with ' "pick-isses", "twobills", crowbars and shovels' and 'the interest of the parish was concentrated on this wonderful "path" which was to go down the face of a dangerous cliff, from nowhere in particular to nobody knew where! ... There was much triumph when the work was completed. An opening day was arranged and a party of twenty visitors descended the dizzy path and were introduced to the wonders of the new-found caves.'

Despite many narrow escapes James and a college friend, called Morrell, set themselves to 'conquer the Champion climb amongst the natives, where the cliffs descend to the sea in sheer precipitous walls of three and four hundred feet.' We think this Champion Climb was The Claw.
In 1875, after five years in North Devon, James Hannington became Curate-in-Charge of St. George's, Hurstpierpoint, Sussex, a family living. In 1882, he volunteered for service in Africa with the Church Missionary Society and within two years, on 24th June, 1884, aged 37, he was ordained First Bishop of Eastern Equatorial Africa.

Having lost none of his spirit of adventure, he planned to open a hazardous new route into Uganda. On 29th October, 1885, near Lake Victoria Nyanza, he and his companions were murdered by the eighteen-year-old King. One of the first Christian Martyrs of Uganda, he is buried in Kampala Cathedral. In 1938 and 1939 respectively, the Bishop Hannington Memorial Church, Hove, and the Hannington Memorial near Jinja were built.

Martinhoe has its own Hannington Memorial Hall and a stained-glass window, in Combe Martin Parish Church, shows Hannington standing in front of the cliff scenery he loved. James Hannington's zigzag paths are still visible in the heather on the slopes below the Coast Path. We have found, and used, other paths descending the cliffs of Martinhoe Parish, most likely also dug out by 'Mad Jim' and his mates.

B.   E. A. NEWELL ARBER 1870 - 1918

Edward Alexander Newell Arber, MA, ScD, FGS, FLS, was born on August 5th, 1870. He studied Botany and Geology at Trinity College, Cambridge and became Demonstrator in Palæobotany, University of Cambridge from 1899-1918. He was a Founder Member of the Sedgwick Museum of Geology, Cambridge. According to his obituary in the Cambridge Journal 1918, his contribution to the science of Geology is considered to consist chiefly in 'the application of palæobotanical evidence to the problems of geological structure'.

In Newell Arber's letters he writes, 'My mania is quite a modest one. It is a desire to visit every single spot in this country where fossil plants have ever been found. To gain that full power of knowledge which can only be got by having been to the place, seen it, photographed it and collected from it. When you have done this you have a "grip" which is masterly.' And in another letter, 'I have had a bad attack of the West (Devon) a calling ... It gets worse and is getting beyond my control.'

From 1903, Arber made twelve geological expeditions to North Devon, to determine the age of the local sedimentary rocks by means of their fossils. He confirmed that the 'building blocks' of Exmoor were formed in the Lower Devonian Age. His study, *The Coast Scenery of North Devon*, is described by Eric Robinson of the Geologists' Association as 'an early venture in coastal geomorphology'. The difficulties of the work were extreme and Newell Arber says he soon found himself distracted from fossil flora plants and worms by the dramatic sea-cliffs and their waterfalls. He could see plainly that the

horizontal beds of sediment, once the floor of a lake or shallow sea, had been tilted up by mountain-building forces.

Along the Exmoor Coast the sea had exposed *strata*, dipping sometimes north and sometimes south, with some strata folded and contorted, and some strata standing vertically up on end. Newell Arber realised that these sloping strata determined the shape of the Exmoor cliffs.

Hilltop weathering of the *scarp-face* had created the steep coastal slope, while the sea had eroded the lower section into vertical cliffs. Arber called this profile hog's-back, as distinct from the flat-top profile of the Hartland cliffs. He also noted that the waterfalls, at Woody Bay, Hollow Brook, Holelake and Sherracombe, were near-vertical because they flowed north: that is in the opposite direction to the southern *dip-slope* of the bedrock.

Newell Arber considered that the shore between Woody Bay and Combe Martin was inaccessible, except by boat. He hired a Combe Martin boat and crew, who rowed him as far as Heddon's Mouth, putting him ashore at Sherracombe along the way. His future wife, Agnes Robertson, PhD, FRS (Gold Medallist, first Botanist and third woman overall to be elected to the Royal Society) in her diary of 1910, gives a delightful description of one of their boat adventures along the coast from Combe Martin to Heddon's Mouth. It would appear, from Newell's annotated six-inch map, that he had descended the Holelake stream, but sadly could not reach the beach there and never saw the magnificent waterfall in spate. His work has set the pattern for all later exploration, as this book endeavours to show.

C. MURIEL AGNES ARBER 1913 - 2004

Muriel Agnes Arber, MA, Cantab, geologist and teacher, only child of Newell and Agnes Arber, was born in Cambridge on 21st July, 1913. Her parents met when both were Demonstrators at University College, London. Muriel was proud to tell how their wedding was 'conducted and geologically sealed' by the renowned Revd. Professor Thomas G. Bonney. The consulting fees her father earned, by applying his knowledge of palaeobotany to stratigraphy, had allowed them to marry and Muriel often remarked: 'I owe my existence to the Kent Coalfields!' Her Godmother was the British morphologist, Ethel Sergant (1863 -1918).

Muriel Arber studied English, then Natural Sciences at Newnham College, graduating in Geology. She later did research on strophomenid brachiopods at the Sedgwick Museum, under the supervision of the palæobotanist, Oliver M.B. Bulman. This led to three detailed published papers but the work was unpaid. She published a succession of papers on the geomorphology of North Devon and Lyme Regis coastal areas, with special reference to sea level change, cliff profiles and the active land-slipping. Her mother, Agnes, in her last publication, *The Manifold and the One*, 1957, pays her the following tribute: 'Finally I wish to record how much I owe to joint "hammering out" of day-to-day experience and of the ideas that came our way with my daughter Muriel - a process which at its happiest moments yields enkindling sparks.'

Elected to the Council of the Geologists' Association, serving as Vice President and then as President (1972 –73), Muriel Arber became First President of the Friends of the Sedgwick Museum in 2003.

At the age of three, she had literally followed in her father's footsteps to the Sedgwick Museum. When asked where she had been, she announced, 'Father showed me round the Museum but I don't actually work there!' She was only five when he died, at the age of 48, but his research into the origin of the hog's-back cliffs was to inspire her for the rest of her life. In 1969 she was responsible for the reprint of his book *The Coast Scenery of North Devon*. Her Presidential Address to the Geologists' Association, in 1974, was titled *The Cliffs of North Devon*. It was with deep regret to all who knew her that she died before she could publish this research in more detail. In 1992 a supper and a lecture on The Hidden Edge of Exmoor was given in her honour at the Museum of North Devon, Barnstaple. In 2002 she was given the Freedom of the Borough of Lyme Regis, as its 'oldest tourist'.

When we first met this remarkable lady she had been coming down to North Devon practically every year since before the Second World War. She came first with her mother and then alone, staying at the Imperial Hotel in Barnstaple. Nicknamed by our children 'The Muriel Hotel', we would meet her there on arrival and, over tea and biscuits, plan her trips on Exmoor and along the coast she loved. She took great delight, especially as an octogenarian, to be taken off the 'mere tourist path', on a safety rope, to stand where her father most certainly must have stood with his stand camera and glass plates to take his photographs and make notes.

Family photographs bear evidence that from 1980 Muriel was 'family' to us. Many of them show her familiar figure seated on what the children called 'a Muriel', a nice smooth slab of rock, just the right height for her to sit on and rise up again with dignity. Many photographs show her striding alone, stopping every now and again to make records, her shoulders slung with bags containing her camera and notebook, her Geological Survey and 6" Ordnance Survey maps, her spyglass, compass, mobile phone and her precious manuscript: all remaining determinedly in place, even for lunch or tea - ever the working Geologist!

It gave Muriel profound satisfaction to learn that Kester had taken up her father's challenge, had actually completed it, and that the whole family was now engaged in exploring the Exmoor cliffs. She was one of our most enthusiastic supporters when, in the 1980s, Kester decided to make a complete photographic record in colour, of what is now called the *Exmoor Coast Traverse*. Her knowledge and insight into North Devon's geological structure has been invaluable, and a profound influence also on Kester's drawing and landscape painting. One of the last things Muriel was able to write with her own hand was the Foreword for this book: for this encouragement we will always be profoundly grateful.

D. CLEMENT ARCHER 1902 – 1967

Tim Webb with Jeanne Brimson and Clement Archer

Clement H. Archer, a Himalayan mountaineer from West Somerset, known as Clemmie, was the first to take up Newell Arber's challenge of 1908. Fifty years later, in 1958, he made it his own Everest Expedition. He started with the 'easy-bits', walking miles of boulder beaches looking, at regular intervals along the cliff, for safe ways down and escape routes up.

Clemmie and his companion, Cecil Agar of Ilfracombe, were helped by Dr. Ernest Mold of Lynton, who kindly and happily sailed his little *picarooner* boat close under the steep cliffs, west of Lynmouth. From this boat, Clemmie could spy out the lower end of potential cliff routes and match them to his cliff-top observations.

Using traditional mountaineering techniques and Alpine equipment Clemmie set about establishing steep, sometimes vertical, routes down to remote beaches. His *tricouni* nailed boots were ideal for steep turf, and his long handled ice-axe was excellent for getting a 'bite' on Exmoor's unstable edge. He designed *super-pitons*, some three feet long, which were cut out of angle-iron by Bert Kerslake, the Washford blacksmith.

With lump hammers Clemmie drove them into the cliff and with difficulty tied on his stiff hawser-laid rope; very cumbersome when wet. He then wound a waist-length rope around himself and clipped onto the *abseil* rope with heavy iron *karabiners*. For 'tricky' ascents of the fixed rope he used the traditional *prusik-loop* system.

Clemmie Archer was a tall, ambling man, eccentric, pedantic and impatient. It was a terrifying experience to be driven by him at high speed across Exmoor, but it was even more terrifying to be with him on an exposed cliff. First he would not be able to find a *belay*, then his rope would tangle, then he would lose his temper completely, cursing and swearing. Once he threw his rope into the sea and it was left to 'Sherpa' Kester, to *solo* the final descent and rescue it from the swell.

Safely down on the beach Clemmie would have a long drink of beer, sometimes supplemented by an amber liquid which he explained 'contained salt to replace sweat!'. His nailed boots, designed for snow and ice, were useless on smooth sea-worn rock and he sometimes fell over in a shower of sparks and expletives, one of which gave 'Bloody Beach!' its name. He solved the problem by changing to his Wellington boots, in which he had carried his beer bottles. Horizontal progress was then a mixture of boulder-hopping and creeping along reefs and ledges.

Archer's method of avoiding vertical rock was simply to walk, fully clothed, into the sea. Using his long ice-axe as a walking-stick-cum-depth-probe, up to his chest amongst big boulders, he would sometimes have 'to swim for it'. He often spent hours soaked to the skin. We occasionally find a discarded beer bottle and his distinctive super-pitons (not now in use) as we follow in his footsteps.

With fellow mountaineer, Cecil Agar, Clemmie took five years to complete Newell Arber's Exmoor Challenge. They proved it was possible to penetrate the precipitous landscape and 'walk the beach' from Foreland Point to Combe Martin; albeit with occasional wet feet. In 1961, Archer published, privately, a detailed account of his explorations below the sea-cliffs from Woody Bay to Combe Martin.

In 1963 he gave a two-hour lecture at the Queen's Hall, Barnstaple, with only a map to illustrate his achievement! In 1964, Cyril and Pat Manning, of Barnstaple, joined him for another season of expeditions but during 1965 Clemmie fell and broke his leg at Lymcove. Cyril saved his life, but he never climbed again. He died two years later in 1967.

Modern rock-climbers, who follow in Clemmie Archer's footsteps, may do it quicker and with more style but they are amazed and full of admiration at what he was able to achieve with basic pre-Second World War mountaineering equipment.

After Clemmie Archer's Queen's Hall talk, politely applauded, only two people emerged from the audience to respond: Cyril and Pat Manning. It turned out that they knew the Martinhoe cliffs intimately and also excelled at rock-climbing out on the cliffs. They joined forces to tackle those parts 'unsatisfactorily resolved', where Archer had had to wade, or even swim. Cyril Manning turned out to be a sort of Devonian rock-gymnast in army boots. He moved so gracefully across vertical rock faces that he made it look easy. Pat's acute sense of balance enabled her to follow him in total confidence. She recalls that she nearly always went with him because: 'When I saw where he went it was easier to go with him than to wait for him to come home!'

'I did several expeditions with them,' Archer wrote, 'and found their climbing standards higher than my own. We did magnificently successful expeditions together, some of these climbs were the best I have ever done. The credit for the discovery of the new dry-shod routes belongs to Cyril Manning.'

Cyril Manning was the RSPB Warden for Chapel Wood, Spraecombe, until his death at 85 years. He was probably best known in North Devon for his interest in the seabird colonies that inhabit Martinhoe parish. His authoritative talks, illustrated by slides, were given on winter evenings, all over the district in the 1970s and 1980s. In the spring he gave talks from the prow of 'Baleana', the Oxenham family boat, which sailed close under the sea-cliffs from Lynmouth. Cyril also led groups, mostly of ladies, down the precipitous cliff paths to Wringapeak; just as James Hannington had done one hundred years before. He talked about his beloved guillemots, razorbills and kittiwakes, from the stone shelter cairn he and Pat built on the top of Wringapeak. They saw the arrival of fulmars on Exmoor, saw the first fulmar chicks fly and were delighted with their successful colonisation along the coast. The story of our Bird Count Expeditions is given in the Appendix.

In the 1980s Cyril generously shared with us his knowledge of Exmoor. He would have liked to have been out climbing the cliffs, exploring abandoned mine-workings and collecting minerals every day, but as Workshop Foreman at the County Garage, he often had to work six days a week. He made his own rock pitons, filing the threads out of half-inch nuts and welding them to eight-inch metal blades. He found that Landrover half-shafts made excellent super-pitons for *abseiling*. Any Landrover that came in with transmission noise had new half-shafts fitted. Cyril confessed that an engineer from the Landrover factory once came enquiring why Exmoor terrain did more damage to axles than the foothills of the Himalayas!

Helen Harris, Cyril's step-daughter, writes for this book: 'I started going out to the cliffs with Cyril from the age of about seven. Although it felt like an adventure, it also became a normal weekend activity for us. It was only much later that I realised and appreciated just how unusual and formative an experience it had been. I remember the sense of excitement and anticipation when there was a particularly low tide (our weekend events always seemed to be organised according to the tides and weather). Very low tides not only enabled us to get past difficult points but were also an opportunity to discover things rarely uncovered or seen, e.g. sea urchins and starfish, or shoals of mackerel trapped in deep ponds. There was one particular occasion as a teenager, when I remember being aware of our vulnerability and the potential dangers of our activities. We had entered the roof of a cave through a narrow gap between boulders at the back of a beach and then *chimneyed* down to the sandy floor of the cave below. There was only a very narrow period of time to get out of the cave and round the corner before the tide turned. Due to the inaccessibility of these cliffs any miscalculation could be fatal but fortunately Cyril's knowledge and experience always saved the day.'

Given the opportunity, Cyril Manning could have been a world-class rock-climber. His athletic ability and local knowledge was certainly an inspiration to local explorers, especially to Clemmie Archer, Terry Cheek and the Webb family.

Cyril Manning with Kester Webb and Terry Cheek, 1992

F. TERRY CHEEK

Another rock-gymnast and dedicated explorer of the Exmoor Coast is Terry Cheek, of West Somerset. The young Terry started climbing in 1963, in North Wales, 'in nails and improvised kit, but moved with the times, switching to new equipment as it became available'. 1970 technical innovations meant that everything became lightweight. *Kernmantle* ropes, alloy belay gadgets, hip harnesses and new-fangled rock-boots helped Terry to establish rock-climbing routes up to E2 grade. Terry's local playground is Hurlestone Point. With others from the Taunton Climbing Club, he pioneered over twenty *graded rock-climbs* at Hurlestone, several sea-cliff routes at the Valley of Rocks and five at the Little Hangman. Clemmie Archer was Terry's neighbour at Torre, near Washford. A keen meteorologist, as well as an explorer, Clemmie kept several weather stations. He often took Terry, as a young teenager, to record the data collected up on Exmoor, but thought him too young to take out on the cliffs!

On his website Terry writes: 'I decided to join the army as a boy soldier at 15 years old. Clemmie was a retired colonel and gave me a good reference. I joined the battalion's climbing club to learn technique. I returned home in 1968 and found that Clemmie had fallen below Trentishoe and broken his leg. In 1974, I became an instructor at the Police Cadet Training Centre in Taunton. In 1976 I met up with Cyril Manning on the Exmoor Coast and quickly realised that I would have to ignore quite a lot of what I had been taught about correct climbing procedures, if I was going to keep up with this man who was older than my father. Cyril's technique was bred of necessity. The tide

Terry Cheek

waits for no man. Here was a place of awe-inspiring scenery, with huge cliffs and massive waves, with only a six-hour window to achieve your goal. Speed and knowledge are the key. I quickly got up to speed and with knowledge of the escape routes, twenty pioneered by Cyril himself, I began to feel at ease. Cyril told me of his adventures with Clemmie Archer and how The

Traverse Route had been pieced together over the years. He lent me his copy of Archer's rare guidebook.'

The first incident Terry remembers on the Exmoor Cliffs was at Coney Combe, during 1967. The Climber Magazine had published an article on 'ash wooden wedges for bashing into cracks that were too wide to take pitons'. He decided to try out the wedges at Hurlestone and climbed thirty feet up a route now called 'Fools and Corpses'. With his cousin, Rodney Watts, holding the rope below, he placed a wedge, clipped into it and jumped off. He remembers skidding past Rodney on the grass slope, having first tumbled down the slab with the wedge banging him on the head.

He was unhurt but had ripped out the seat of his trousers and had to make an ignominious way back to the car park with his pullover carefully hiding the damage to his rear.

One of Terry's greatest achievements came in 1978, when he led a team of three police cadets, in a single-push, dry-shod expedition from Foreland Lighthouse to Combe Martin Harbour. It took four and a half days; climbing sometimes at night and sleeping on the beaches during high tide. The team had to carry its own equipment and be entirely self-sufficient. Terry's own account of this expedition is given in the Appendix.

Terry is known for his generosity and patience, leading and helping other explorers to tackle the Traverse. A born instructor, his detailed knowledge of the terrain and where to set up the safest belays has benefited so many, from Mollie Rodber to Martin Crocker and especially two generations of the Webb family.

Kester and Elizabeth Webb in the company of Cyril Manning on the Exmoor cliffs with a backdrop of the Valley of Rocks and the Foreland.

G. KESTER WEBB AND FAMILY

In the 1950s, as teenagers, my brother Tim and I were often out, cycling all over Exmoor and the Brendon Hills. We explored the coast, looking for birds' nests and scrambling about the cliffs, creeping into sea-caves and generally enjoying the whole delightful place. Later on in the 1960s, Tim's future wife, Jeanne Brimson, of Old Cleeve, Somerset, came along to visit several of the 'desperate to get at places'. In the autumn of 1963, when Cyril Manning developed a bad knee, Clemmie Archer turned to me for help in developing access and escape routes for the more inhospitable sections.

We were hardly climbing companions. Over forty years younger than Archer, I was regarded as merely some sort of 'Sherpa in monkey boots'. He never discussed his overall agenda with me, or mentioned Newell Arber's challenge, he just loaded me up with stiff rope, angle-iron and garden tools. I had to remember my place and never lead a route. Occasionally I did have to take the initiative, if only to avert disaster.

While Clemmie was hospitalised following his accident, Tim, Jeanne and I successfully tackled the difficult rock-traverse at Lymcove Point. Clemmie called this 'The Swim', as he always had to take to the sea there. His records acknowledge only the 'Brothers Webb' for this traverse; perhaps he could not admit to himself that a woman had done what he had had 'to funk'.

It was not until 1969 that I went on expeditions with Cyril and Pat Manning; after I met Elizabeth Hibbett, when we were both lecturing in Bristol. The Mannings shared their skills, knowledge and enthusiasm with us in the same generous way they had done with Clemmie, and with many other people interested in the coast, geologists and ornithologists, as well as climbers. We remember some very enjoyable expeditions together, especially around the Little Hangman and into The 'Inner Sanctuary'.

On one occasion, while I was looking for a suitable belay for our safety rope, I saw my future wife disappearing after Cyril, entirely ropeless down over the cliff edge onto the '*Flying Buttress*': such confidence did he inspire!

I had been working, in the 1960s, as a professional photographer; sometimes assisting the features writer, Peter Hesp, of the Somerset County Gazette. Peter accompanied me on a few expeditions and was more patient than most fellow climbers who are not usually inclined to wait for photographers. If I pointed a lens in his direction, Clemmie Archer always turned his back.

As my wife was an energetic rock-gymnast and also quite accustomed by this time to being photographed 'for scale' in precipitous locations, I had the idea of re-enacting the whole Exmoor Traverse. The making of a complete visual record became my hobby from then on. Our daughter Rebekah and son Martin did not start climbing seriously with us until after they were ten years

Liz and Rebekah Webb at Wringapeak with cousin Simon Webb, 1975

old; but Pat and Cyril were only mildly surprised to see the two-month-old Rebekah in her *Karrimor sling*, at the cairn on the top of Wringapeak.

In 1973 the scramble down was a bit easier than it is now. Exploring became the pattern of our life as a family and we even held surprise Birthday Parties for the children and their friends in the caves, complete with cake, candles and balloons. As both children record, they were so young they were not aware of the first time they were introduced to the Traverse.

Martin Webb on a Coastguard Exercise

They grew up thinking that 'going to the beach' meant walking down hundreds of feet of coastal slope, *abseiling* the last hundred feet of cliff, to play amongst cold boulders where perhaps no human foot had ever trod. And as the tide came in, the only way home for them was sometimes a *jumar* rope-climb and always a long trudge back up to the Coast Path.

Mountaineering 'horizontally and in reverse' does not attract many and even seasoned climbers find the level of exposure, above moving water, difficult at first. Rebekah and Martin seemed unaffected and because of their slight weight they put adults to shame with their climbing and abseiling skills.

Tackling Newell Arber's challenge became a very necessary escape from the world of work. Facing the extremes of the Exmoor Coast focuses the mind on what is important in life, it renews energy and gives great personal satisfaction.

In 2005, Liz, at 67, became the first woman to 'set up a climb' on the Exmoor Coast at Hurlestone; seconded by Terry Cheek she called it 'Roller Coaster' (180 ft *HVD* Hard Very Difficult with three pitches). Its switchback character may be viewed on Terry Cheek's *Exmoor Walker* and on 'U Tube' websites.

In all, it took us four years to make a comprehensive photographic record of *The Exmoor Coast Traverse* and I have been upgrading, and adding to it with aerial photography ever since. My talks, under the title *The Hidden Edge of Exmoor*, now occupy my time during the winter months at venues all over Somerset and Devon.

Rebekah writes for this book: *'The joy of walking the South West Coast Path, breathing in the fresh sea air and admiring the dramatic scenery, is a big part of my life. I have my parents to thank for this as it was they who led me along the Hidden Edge of Exmoor years before my memory can stretch. I am told I was only months old when I took my first foray along the cliff edges. So perhaps it is no wonder that this coast is where I naturally feel at home. Exmoor has some stunning scenery. I am privileged to have witnessed first-hand some of its 'special places', places hidden and completely inaccessible to most. I am proud of my parents' achievements, their life-long enthusiasm for this amazing traverse and for gathering their stories, memories and photographs of this magical place into this special monograph.'*

Right: Rebekah Webb climbing Hurlestone with Terry Cheek in 1993.
Below: Martin Webb traversing Yes Tor with Philip Osborne.

Martin thoroughly enjoyed exploring as a child and is still an adventure-climber, accompanying Terry Cheek on the Traverse. He too can never remember being introduced to the place:-

'It seemed always there. Even if I live away I will always regard this coast as my home. It's the wilderness that makes it special. There is something so precious about this place.'

H. MORE EXPLORERS

We have organised over a hundred expeditions with our family and friends, during the course of twenty-five years. In 1985 a Climbing Club was set up in Barnstaple by an enthusiastic fellow explorer, Trevor Karslake. Some of its members were eager to help us record the whole of the Exmoor Traverse and joined in our weekend expeditions. All who came with us, in the next five years, feature somewhere in the photographic record. Simon Bell recalls, '... lots of happy memories, the sense of excitement abseiling down to a hidden beach, the quiet and peace down there, climbing along ledges just a few feet above the waves, those caves and gullies that few had ventured to and the privilege of being part of an exclusive group of visitors to those inaccessible places.'

To qualify for completion of Newell Arber's Challenge, explorers have to traverse the fifteen miles of shoreline from Foreland Point to Combe Martin. With parties of up to ten people we started with the easy bits of open foreshore and rock scrambles and only the occasional awkward 'move'. As we struggled with more sustained stretches of serious climbing, with exposure above the moving sea, the gang mysteriously dwindled! The expeditions were usually a pleasant day out, but sometimes, despite careful planning, an outing could turn into 'an epic'; with climbing to Severe grade necessary, in order to deal with the unexpected. Sometimes a few of us slept out overnight at Hollow Combe or in remote limekilns to catch the sunrise. There was always a great sense of camaraderie and a touching sense of trust in the 'leaders'.

The over-riding memory of these expeditions was the sense of achievement. We were experiencing a most extraordinary adventure right here on Exmoor.

Alan Tringham abseiling on Yes Tor

Yogi Hole, Hollow Brook: Left to Right:
Brian Pearce, Philip Draper, Peter Upstone, Simon Bell,
Chris Jones, Mike Harris, Steve Bennett, Rob Jones.

From left to right:
Adrian Cheek, Clare Tryon, Terry Cheek, Jon Smith, Martin Webb, Kester Webb, Elizabeth Webb

Sitting left to right: Liz Webb, Martin Webb and Rebekah Webb
Standing left to right: Philip Osborne, Jon Smith, David Jenkins, David Taylor,
Ian Walker, Clare Tryon, Kester Webb.

Above: Little Burland Rocks; an expedition to Hannington's Cave & The Claw (1992).

Philip Osborne   David Hillebrandt   Jon Smith   Michael Nix   Keith Muncey   Terry Cheek
                                                Kes Webb   Alan Worth
    Clare Tryon   Harriet Bridle   Liz Webb   Adrian Cheek
                                                                      Cyril Manning   Ben

The following climbers 'can boast a remarkable record', having completed the Exmoor Traverse from the Foreland Point to Combe Martin starting in the year:-

1954: Clement Archer, Cecil Agar.
1959: Kester Webb, Tim Webb.
1964: Cyril Manning, Pat Manning.
1969: Elizabeth Webb née Hibbett.
1967: Terry Cheek.
1978: One-Push Expedition. Terry Cheek with Police Cadets: Robert Simmonds, Graham Rodgers, Trevor Simpson.
1984: Martin Webb, David Taylor, Philip Osborne, Clare Tryon, Rob Jones, Jimmy Woolmington.
1995: Mollie Rodber (at 70 yrs).
2006: Mark Padgett, Becky Padgett.

The following have partly completed the Exmoor Traverse starting in the year:-

1961: Jeanne Webb née Brimson.
1968: Alan Tringham.
1973: Rebekah Webb.
1985: Steve Bennett, Philip Draper, Chris Jones, David Jenkins, Martin Blunt, Stuart Shell, Jim Pinn, Jon Smith, Chris Jones, Mike Harris, Trevor Karslake, Peter Upstone, Amanda Barton.

Right: Traversing the Great Bastion: Clare Tryon, Terry Cheek, David Hillebrandt, Martine Scholle

THE EXMOOR TRAVERSE
A Geographical Description from East to West

1. MINEHEAD: Behind North Hill

The traveller, looking west from Dunster Marshes, sees the Exmoor Hills dramatically terminated by the bulbous profile of North Hill. This steep north face plunges seaward down to Minehead Harbour, guarding whatever mysteries lie behind and beyond. *The Exmoor Coast Traverse* begins beneath the steep wooded slopes of North Hill, just west of the Harbour at the National Park Boundary.

Here the shoreline is a shifting bank of grey pebbles and boulders that continues for fourteen miles, with only occasional sandy respites, all the way to the Foreland Point in North Devon. Half a mile west of the harbour is a patch of sand, below the vertical face of Culvercliffe. This seventy-foot high sea-cliff is a splendid *exposure* of the Devonian *Sandstones*, that are the building blocks of northern Exmoor. Traditionally called *'Hangman Grits'*, by Newell Arber et al., these sedimentary deposits are now referred to as the *'Hangman Sandstone Formations'* in British Geological Survey publications.

At Culvercliffe the sandstones are clearly visible, with horizontal beds folded down at 90° at the western end of the exposure. To the landscape artist, the Culvercliffe looks like a huge mural painted with flat brushes. The rock wall is coloured with purples, reds and pinks whilst down near sea level the surface is decorated with bands of yellow lichens. The cliff is then topped off with vegetation and trees in a variety of greens with a variety of textures.

The stone walls of a V-shaped fish weir are visible on the sand at the lowest tides.

Culvercliffe Beach with stone fish weir

28

The sandstone rock face exposure at Culvercliffe

Beyond Culvercliffe, the ridged-up banks of grey pebbles curve out around the delta-shaped spread of Greenaleigh Meadows. This isolated farmstead, hidden behind North Hill, is in a most attractive setting. Surrounded by trees, the green field descends to a little lagoon protected by the pebble ridge, and over on the seaward side is a small sandy beach. All too soon for the explorer the sand gives way to a litter of huge boulders.

Above the low crumbling cliffs the vegetated slopes reach up to the Rugged Path at the 600 ft contour. Within the next half mile are three steep valleys, with streams cascading down onto the rocky shore, all with colourful and evocative names. The first is Burgundy Chapel, followed by Bramble Combe. The last and biggest is Grexy Combe, which rises up by Furzebury Brake and carves itself a dramatic little ravine for its last hundred yards plunge to the sea. Between Grexy Combe and Henners Combe there are no streams or landmarks, only a laborious plod over boulders; a distance of two miles, that feels more like three to any beach walker. Above is a huge area of uniformly north-dipping slope, covered by landslips and *scree*, known as the Eastern and Western Brockholes.

At the eastern flank of Henners Combe the shoreline bends slightly more to the west around the wave-washed headland of Minehead *Bluff*. This seventy-foot outcrop, of near vertical sandstone slabs, is where Terry Cheek, seconded by Clare Tryon, set up 'Terrigrin', the most easterly of all Exmoor's graded climbs.

Minehead Bluff offers a fine view westward along the mountainous shoulders of Selworthy Beacon, guarding the finest sand beach in all of Somerset - Selworthy Sands.

29

Vegetated coastal slopes with screes and landslips below Brock Holes

Camouflaged Auster at Five Sisters Slabs (EFW).

2. SELWORTHY SANDS

At low tide Selworthy Sands stretches for three-quarters of a mile, with firm flat sand at the eastern end. Most of the beach is deeply grooved with swirling patterns of sandy ridges and meandering pools, sculpted by the strong tidal currents streaming from the tip of Hurlestone Point. They are exposed for only four hours or so at low tide, and the turning tide comes in swiftly to cover the beach; by half-tide the sand has usually disappeared.

Selworthy Sand is not visible on the Coast Path, which goes inland of Hurlestone. Access is difficult. Rock-climbers and scramblers often use the oblique Gull Hole at the west end of the beach, which is tidal.

The fisherman's route down a hundred feet of giant scree is eroded and unstable. The beach is very special to the determined few who go there: four or five dedicated fishermen at most, explorers on the Traverse and the occasional stray tourist. Mollie and the late Neville Rodber, of Minehead, were regular climbing visitors. The Search and Rescue Services usually approach from the sea for their 'familiarisation exercises'.

One elderly man from Porlock told how, years ago, he had walked and scrambled along the beach from Porlock Weir to Lynmouth, using several low tides. We asked whether he had tried the much easier 'beach crawl' going east to Minehead. 'Oh no, you can't go that way!' he said, 'You see, Selworthy Sands is sinking sands, you could get stuck and then drowned when the tide came in.'

All the old villagers warned me about the sinking sands!' No doubt that warning has been handed down for generations, ever since the heyday of local smugglers, who wanted this beach and its extensive dry caves all to themselves: the best smuggling beach of all the twenty-four miles of Exmoor Coast.

Halfway along the Sands, the pools of brackish water reflect the five slabs of overlapping rock that recline against the unstable coastal slopes. These 'Five Sisters' dip steeply north, making a wave-like profile.

The Climbing Guide records that it was here Liz Hibbett Webb, seconded by Terry Cheek, set up 'Roller Coaster'. The parallel climb on 'Terry's Slabs' is called 'Turf Wars'; out of Terry's frustration with the encroaching vegetation.

The views from the beach are some of the finest on all Exmoor. Looking back east, towering above is the distinctive cone of Henners Hill, whose northern ridge descends five hundred feet to Minehead Bluff. Then comes the deep 'V' of Henners Combe, with its white cascade. Looking south and inland is the mountainous north face between Henners Combe and East Combe.

In the middle distance, to the west, the silhouette of the old Coastguard building stands stark on the ridge of Hurlestone, above the smooth-layered slabs of Eastern Cliffs. To the far west, beyond the white surf, are the blue hills of Culbone and Countisbury.

Overleaf: Selworthy Sands, Henner's Combe and Minehead Bluff

Slabs of Eastern Cliffs at Sunset

Towards the western end of Selworthy Sands, where the ubiquitous boulders take over again, a dry *hanging valley* reveals itself above a one hundred foot scree slope. This strange 'U' shaped valley, choked with broken rock and known as Coney Combe, is abruptly terminated by a flat inland rock-face, reminiscent of a Welsh mountain *cwm*. Exposed slabs of fine Hangman Grits, standing up on end and striking due east-west, create an imposing 150 ft high wall parallel with the shoreline. In the centre of this wall is a large, circular, stepped recess, where two-foot thick slabs have been levered out, probably by ice. This weird geological feature is the location of a dozen graded climbs set up by local lads, including Terry Cheek and Simon Mooney. This recess has enlarged itself recently: a large chunk of a long established *rock-route* has disconcertingly joined the broken debris on the floor of Coney Combe!

Below Coney Combe, the stretch of unstable sea-cliff suddenly gives way to solid curved bedrock. Their dip to the north steepens, with overlapping slabs of smooth rock building higher and higher and reaching nearly to Hurlestone Point itself. The cliff face here is unusual; convex at the eastern end, a mixture of concave and convex slabs in the middle and then concave at the western end. Behind the cliff face at sea level softer strata have been eroded, creating tall, thin, slot-shaped caves and watery corridors parallel with the shore.

The Red Slab Climbing Club of Taunton started putting up routes at Hurlestone in 1963, with the traverse of Fledgling Wall and Borrowmere in 1971. The latter route is the reason why so many of the later routes have names from The Lord of the Rings. Terry Cheek began rock-climbing there in 1973: beginning with climbs on the lower Fledgling Wall and working up to Coastguard Wall. This latter slab is large and smooth; standing up at 75°, it is a challenging 190 ft in height. Of the thirty graded rock-climbs on the Eastern Cliffs, nine of them are on Coastguard Wall. The beach below here is a jumble of awkward boulders, leading towards a dark gully that rises up to the eastern entrance of the Gull Hole.

Hurlestone Point in the light of dawn

Liz Webb on Coastguard Wall, Hurlestone

Curving strata of the Western Cliffs showing the arched roof of the Gull Hole Thru cave

Hurlestone Western Cliffs

Hurlestone Point, sometimes spelt 'Hurlstone' and on early maps 'Hurtstone', has rock-walls facing north, west and south. Above Coastguard Wall stands the afore-mentioned abandoned Coastguard building, perched on the rocky ridge that sweeps down from Bossington Hill. The ridge tapers as it descends, forming a sharp headland poking out into the sea. It looks, from the air, like a huge fossilized dragon.

The top jaw of this monster is formed by a graceful *anticline* and, at the centre of the arch, some seven beds of rock have been punched right through by the sea, leaving a twelve-foot, and very draughty, *thru-cave*. This Gull Hole, with arched ceiling and convex floor, provides an easy half-tide passage from Eastern Cliffs and Selworthy Sands through to Western Cliffs and Bossington Beach. At its centre a small *squeeze* or thru-cave goes secretly south, making a dark and narrow short cut to the west.

The spectacular view from inside the Gull Hole, looks due west down a gully to the sea and out across Porlock Bay. Explorers passing through the hole emerge into a different world, the sunny side of Hurlestone Point. Now the shoreline turns left at right angles to the strike of the bedrock; with rock exposed end-on to the Atlantic storms. The vertical wall makes an ideal sunny playground for climbers training for The Hidden Edge. Twenty rock-routes of every grade have been recorded here, since One Way Street was first climbed in 1971.

Western Cliffs suddenly end in a chunky corner buttress. Then the cliff, turning at right angles and heading back inland this time, terminates the eastern end of Bossington Pebble Ridge. A bright wide vista rewards the explorer; with long views up over Dunkery and the wooded coastal slopes that stretch four and a half miles west to Glenthorne. This famous *storm beach* forms a two-mile edge to the Vale of Porlock.

Below right: *The two-mile long storm beach was breached by the sea in October 1996 and has been allowed to develop naturally ever since.*

Above: Inside the Gull Hole arch, a thru-cave at Hurlestone Point.
Left to right: Ivor Sutton, Liz Webb, Terry Lavis and Mollie Rodber.

Bossington Pebble Ridge is easy-going for the explorer. It is interesting to observe the steady increase in the size of the pebbles as they begin to pile up against Porlock Weir; a historic little harbour with old limekilns. These pebbles surround the Harbour and continue past to Gore Point. Here the shoreline turns west and the landscape changes abruptly to densely wooded coastal slopes, rising steadily to the 650 ft contour of Exmoor's northern hills. The water coming down Worthy Combe is Newell Arber's Stream No.1. Further on are the remains of one lonely limekiln and a boathouse called Rockford Cottage. Arber lists fourteen small streams between Porlock and the Foreland Point, noting that they all cut deeply into their valleys. Many of them rise at a thousand feet, with the watershed less than a mile inland, just north of the A39 Turnpike road.

The boulder beach looking west

The Ivy Stone

After passing the ruins of Rockford Cottage, the shoreline is a remarkably straight and uniform boulder beach. For much of this section the strata dip to the north, leading to frequent landslips, a regular hazard. The hog's-back cliffs have only a few feet of vertical face, except for some noteworthy buttresses. The biggest, called The Ivy Stone, is one mile west of Porlock Weir, below Culbone Woods. It blocks the beach except at low spring tides. It is a modest outcrop, seventy feet high, with overlapping slabs dipping steeply seawards; it boasts five of Terry Cheek's graded climbs.

West of The Ivy Stone, a monotonous trudge over abundant beach boulders continues for the next couple of miles. The only landmarks along the way are first, the deep ravine at Twitchen Combe, next a thirty-foot high pinnacle called The Yellow Stone and then the dilapidated masonry of a couple of limekilns.

Eventually the shoreline curves out and bends below Embelle Wood, where an old track comes down to the ruins of small buildings, with a small low tide *strand* nearby. Both were probably made to import coal and limestone and export burnt lime, oak bark and charcoal in centuries gone by. Embelle's pebble ridge is described by Terry as 'a beach-comber's paradise', it always has a rich selection of marine debris.

E.A. Newell Arber, in *The Coast Scenery of North Devon*, describes the rock hereabouts as 'being of the Foreland Grit series, the beds consisting of hard fine-grained sandstone, forming thick beds, with occasional partings of hard *shales* and pebble beds.' The grey sandstones often look pink, red and purplish, especially where they are also stained by iron oxides. The next two and a half miles are punctuated by little streams cascading down rocky ravines.

All the way from Minehead the Traverse has been alongside rock strata sloping down to the

An Auster at Ivy Stone below Culbone Woods (EFW)

north, in a straight uniform coastline; the only exception being Hurlestone Point. West of Embelle Wood there is more variety as the strata twist and turn and stand up on end at Yenworthy Caves. This dramatic vertical structure is a sequence of reddish slabs, alternating with slots, where softer layers have eroded away to create several narrow rectangular caves. The vertical strata continue upward to form an inland cliff face known as 'The Guildhall'.

Glenthorne

Emerging from the Hidden Edge of Exmoor on sunny days, the explorer can be well rewarded as light floods down the deep Glenthorne valley at the County Boundary. Two streams arrive on the beach, one from Yenworthy, the other is Coscombe Water, Newell Arber's Stream No. 8, which ends in an eight-foot waterfall. The ruins of a boathouse and two limekilns are visible at the top of the wide gravel beach. Along the shoreline, approaching Glenthorne, the northerly dip of the strata is disrupted and turns to face west in places to create cliff walls separated by vertical *fissures*.

According to Ben Halliday, former 'Lord of the Manor of Glenthorne', it was a three-day operation for the boats to deliver coal from South Wales. Firstly the ketch 'anchored off', the crew rowed ashore and during low tide they cleared

boulders from the strand. Next day, at early morning high tide, the ketch was brought in and stranded. As the tide receded, a pair of horse-drawn, two-wheel carts came alongside and fifty tons of coal were shovelled up out of the ship's hold. On the third day, at high tide, the ketch would float off again and sail away out to sea.

The Halliday family home was built in this remote valley in the 1830s. One hundred feet above vertical sea-cliffs a platform was dug out for the house and gardens. In spring and summer unusual botanical 'escapees' from the garden blossom in abundance, obviously enjoying the salty habitat.

In August 1908, Newell Arber wrote to his fiancée, Agnes Robertson, describing a walk along the beach westward from Porlock. As the tide came in he had to take to the cliffs and 'in the end my path suddenly landed me on the tennis lawn in front of a palatial mansion, among a party of girls playing tennis who seemed very surprised and indignant. I had to apologise profusely and slink down an elaborate drive, with further explanations at the Lodge of how on earth I got there. On the whole they were fairly decent about it.' As there is only one house in this lonely spot we assume the 'mansion' must have been Glenthorne.

39

Glenthorne, with a grass tennis lawn perched above the sea (PK)

In 1964, some miles further west, three of us had a similar experience. Clemmie Archer had always been anxious that we should not be visible on remote beaches, in case tourists saw us and tried to follow. Consequently we were in the habit of dressing in army camouflage and only went 'down-over' when we thought no one was looking. Archer used a three foot long ice-axe for climbing on steep turf. On this occasion we were carrying shorter versions, modified from army trenching tools of First World War design. At the end of the expedition we were forced up the cliff by the incoming tide and had to fight our way up through dense vegetation, coming out suddenly into a field below a big house. We set off up hill when a bailiff appeared, pointing a shot-gun at us.

He marched us up to the house where a young woman servant ran out and shouted at us in broad Devon about the evils of trespassing. Then the Lord of the Manor appeared; a portly man with a red face and a foreign accent. Presumably alarmed by figures in combat outfit, draped in ropes and carrying ice-axes, he decided we were Russian spies who had landed from a submarine during the night. After more haranguing and shouting, we were escorted up the long drive and out onto the public road by the servant girl, the bailiff with his gun and the Lord of the Manor in his huge American car. Slipping the clutch, he tried to make us run by bumping the backs of our legs.

5. DESOLATE POINT

West of Glenthorne the strata start arching over and leaning in different directions, to create a more indented shoreline and a more varied landscape. The monotony of boulder-hopping along the Glenthorne stretch of the Traverse can be relieved briefly here by walking under the Giant's Rib, a slab of rock forming a low shallow arch. The sea-cliffs rise steadily towards Wingate Combe on the east side of Desolate Point. Deep in this densely wooded valley, three streams join forces to become Arber's Stream No. 9, and the combined waters plunge seventy feet over the cliff, down steep overlapping slabs, to create Wingate Waterfall. 'It is certainly worth a visit, for besides being very pretty, it is one of the finest examples of a hog's-back cliff waterfall to be found on the whole coast,' wrote Newell Arber to Agnes, in 1908. Terry Cheek describes the stream-bed as resembling a Giant Staircase of slippery overlapping slabs, ending in a terrifying water-shoot down over the cliff-top. From far out to sea, when in spate, it is easy to see why sailors would call this waterfall 'The White Lady'.

Wingate Waterfall with Alan Tringham

'Sir Robert's Chair'. High tide, Desolate Point. Dawn. May 2010

Sir Robert's Chair

The bulbous bulk of Desolate Point is a most interesting landmark of shapes, suggesting different images, which no doubt account for the legends connected with it. Formed by sandstone slabs, up on end and curved both ways, it has a dome-shaped nose. When side-lit, in sunshine, this dome looks like the cushioned back of a chair, with rock columns either side to suggest the armrests. Aerial photography certainly helps to 'read' this shape. It is likely that the whole area appeared to sailors like a giant throne, which they called Sir Robert's Chair. Map-makers, however, limit the name to the half-tide pinnacle of rock standing to seaward of the Point.

Sir Robert's Chair. Climbers on top: Terry Cheek and Jimmy Woolmington.

Despite the dark, dank and lonely location, the smooth chair-back has been climbed by Terry Cheek and others, to establish five rock-routes up to two hundred feet in length. The half-tide pinnacle, once an extension of the chair's foot-rest, has a forty-five foot high vertical south face, with a couple of Jimmy Woolmington's rock-routes. Its seawall north face offers an easier way to the top. The beach is enclosed by the western arm of the chair, descending to form the spur, known as Kite's Foot Bluff. This contorted mass of rock has two 'windows', one inside the hollow core of a whale-back fold; both are thru-caves, giving access to the shore line below the 'slabby-slippy slopes' of Desolate Red.

Desolate Red

For the next two miles Arber's 'Foreland Grits' dip to the north and descend six hundred feet from the Coast Path. This area is well named 'Desolate Red' for it is a huge treeless slope, with glistening slabs of bare rock, between patches of mauve scree and red gashes of recent landslips. The beach here is littered with huge blocks that have crashed down from crumbling outcrops hundreds of feet above. One gigantic landslip destroyed a section of the Coast Path and this has created a habitat for scores of Exmoor whitebeam and rowan saplings. The acres of scree are bounded on the west by the long watery groove of Whitebeam Gully. Continuing west, at beach level and far below Desolate Farmhouse, is an outcrop of chunky sandstone slabs, standing up on end and forming interesting walls and corners. The stone is stained with iron in an attractive variety of orange, reds and purplish browns, to create a most colourful scene, especially when the skies are blue.

Slabby Cliffs of Desolate Red

Picnic at Standing Sandstones

6. COUNTISBURY COVE

Masonry Ruins in Countisbury Cove

The chaos of Desolate Red gives way to regular, wooded slopes, below Kipscombe. The trees conceal long water-courses that have cut deep gullies as they descend from the 800 ft contour. Swannel Gully and Pudleap Girt are particularly terrifying places when in spate, with cascades two feet deep, roaring down their ravines and depositing trees and big rocks onto the foreshore.

The long curve of Countisbury Cove shows the first signs of civilisation since leaving Glenthorne. Three hundred feet up, almost hidden in the trees, is Rodney's; originally a lime-burner's cottage. An old packhorse track zigzags down. The lower bends, re-enforced with stone buttresses, lead to several piles of dilapidated masonry, clinging precariously to the cliff-face. There is a small 'half-eaten'

limekiln and a slipway leading on down to a sandy strand: all that is left of Exmoor's most remote lime-burning site.

It is easier walking in the lee of Foreland Point, with long stretches of gravel and even sand. In times past, maybe as far back as the Stone Age, the abundant beach boulders here have come in useful for building a V-shaped fish weir.

There is a rock-roof to walk under, a small version of the Giant's Rib. Arber's Stream No. 14, a waterfall like a filigree curtain, drains the hanging valley of Coddow Combe. 'Those who are interested in the geology of valleys,' wrote Newell Arber, 'should visit the great *cirque* of Coddow Combe.'

Walking close to the towering bulk of the Foreland, one begins to see huge areas of scree on the eastern wall of the headland, tapering down to the sea.

The long boulder beach, that began at Hurlestone Point, is decisively terminated by the solid *wave-cut platforms* of Goat Rock. At this major landmark there is a safe picnic spot, right on the silhouette of the Foreland; it has been visible since rounding Minehead Bluff. Weary boulder-hopping explorers can sit and look back ten miles to the blue hog's-back of Selworthy Beacon, sweeping down to Hurlestone Point.

7. THE FORELAND POINT

At Goat Rock, the northern tip of the Foreland, the terrain changes dramatically. There is no beach, just wave-washed rock above a deep and dangerous tide-race. It is not surprising then, that it was from the Foreland that Clemmie Archer started his Exmoor Traverse in 1960, and Terry Cheek began his non-stop five-day expedition, in 1978.

The bedding-planes dip steeply to the north at 40°, so the cliff builds rapidly up towards the lighthouse, with *ribs* of the hardest rock sweeping down from the vertical face. As they descend north-westwards the ribs change into tapering reefs that slice into the sea like giant teeth. Running out across the beach they are reminiscent of Hartland's Atlantic shore. The explorer is now faced with descending these overhanging scarp edges.

Seven of these ribs have deep watery gullies between them, undercut on the south side. Looking back up between the ribs, the white tower of the lighthouse is just visible two hundred feet above. In the mid-sixties explorers were usually spotted by the lighthouse keeper, who would abseil down enthusiastically to 'save' them. He was quite disappointed when we declined to be 'rescued' or to call in for a cup of tea.

Fortunately the southernmost and biggest rib has a diamond-shaped hole knocked right through it; a welcome relief. This 'window' frames a superb view south-west across Lynmouth Bay with towering cliffs on the left, a bright wide beach ahead, and a backdrop of ancient earthworks on Wind Hill. To the right is the village of Lynmouth, with a glimpse of the Valley of Rocks.

Lynmouth Foreland Lighthouse above reefs

Thru-cave in reef at Foreland Pont. Views west to Valley of Rocks and beyond.

In this dramatic landscape the Traverse proceeds south-west along a wide shore that is exposed to wave-attack from the Atlantic's north-west gales. The hungry sea has excavated a row of seven caves between layers of upright strata. The high-tide surf punches air into these tapering tunnels until the wave energy dissipates; then the compressed air explodes out again, spitting sea-spray. On quiet days the booming noise of the Gun-Chamber Caverns can be heard in Lynmouth.

The contorted strata of the Gun-Chamber Caverns

Great Red; 'a terrifying ravine'. Two small figures in red, centre left, give a sense of scale

The twin villages of Lynton and Lynmouth have a fine view across the bay to the huge hog's-backs of Foreland and Countisbury Hill.

Clearly visible is the green curve of Coddow Slip and the rugged gash of Great Red; a terrifying ravine, cut into a jumble of chaotic iron-stained rock, which narrows and steepens until it is finally 'eating' the turf at the 600 ft contour.

It used to be 'an awesome climb' but Terry Cheek reports that, 'sadly its deep entrance from the beach has been filled with large boulders from a rock-fall hundreds of feet above.'

The truly mountainous terrain of this cliffscape, below Countisbury, is a timely reminder of the sheer scale of *The Hidden Edge of Exmoor.*

Sillery Sands

The sea-cliffs of Hangman sandstones build higher as the strata become more chaotic, with huge *fault-lines* fracturing the hillsides below Countisbury Common. The straight stretch of shore south of Great Red, called Sillery Sands, is divided by the low *bluff* of Upper Blackhead and then again by the strange foreshore pinnacle of Lower Blackhead: a distraction for rock gymnasts passing along on the Traverse.

Another distraction is the sand, for this is a well-loved swimming-beach. It boasts its own rock sphinx, best seen from the zigzag tourist track of fourteen bends up to the Coast Path.

The sand of Sillery Beach ends abruptly at a vertical cliff face, which makes a corner where the shoreline turns west again. Here at Ninney's Well Bay, the Hangman Sandstone Formation is faulted against the Lynton Formation. The fault plane is nearly vertical and short and the hard Hangman Sandstone, that has built the landscape all the way from Minehead, is now lying on the top of rocks called *Lynton Beds*. Newell Arber describes these rocks, which will form the shore for the next five miles, as *grey slates* and *shales*, with inter-bedded *grits* that are often *ripple-marked*. They change the whole character of the beach, for the softer rock is easily sculpted into a variety of half-tide pinnacles; such as those huddled in the corner below Ninney's Well. Then it is only a mile walk from Sillery Sands to the River Lyn.

Sillery Sands Beach

The Valley of Rocks: Mother Meldrum's Gut, 'an awe-inspiring place'.

Again the villages of Lynton and Lynmouth offer good views of a typical Exmoor beach and one of Exmoor's highest sea-cliffs, the Foreland. During the summer months there are also excellent local boat trips to Woody Bay, Heddon's Mouth and Countisbury Cove. When the 'big boats' once called at Lynmouth, there was the excitement of boarding an open boat like *'Belaena'* and 'meeting the steamer' half a mile out at sea. In Victorian times this area was known as 'Little Switzerland', because of the dramatic landscape created by the River Lyn and the Valley of Rocks.

Many have attempted to describe this famous Valley from different vantage-points. The Minehead Memoirs of the British Geological Survey describe the rocks of the Lynton Formations as 'beds of finely laminated fine-grained sandstones and *mudstones*, grey in colour, some beds ripple-marked, some layers containing fossils.' Newell Arber, sitting six hundred feet up on Hollerday Hill, in a 1908 letter to his fiancée, describes them as 'a succession of picturesque ruin-like slabs piled one upon the other forming unbounded masses of natural masonry. The beach is strewn with rectangular and cubical boulders.' It appears that the near horizontal bedding planes and vertical *jointing* cracks have been enlarged by weathering, to create the square blocks and angular cavities that attract rock-climbers. Clemmie Archer, in 1958, thought the 'piles of huge rectangular monoliths' had a 'peculiar grandeur of their own.' Explorers down on the beach may notice that the rectangular structure of the cliffs is echoed in the cuboid shapes of the sea-caves.

Proceeding west from Lynmouth Harbour requires good boulder-hopping technique and the stamina to keep going for at least a quarter of a mile. Many of the stones are the size of cars, many rectangular and some boldly ripple-marked. Below Middle Gate, up in the Valley of Rocks, the beach tapers until the boulders give way to horizontal wave-cut platforms and ever-narrowing ledges, leading to a series of chunky buttresses with narrow inlets between their steep walls.

A small, fifty-foot, pillar-like buttress forms the sheer east wall of the East Inlet Gully, which only dries out on a low tide with no sea-swell. 'The climb into the back of this gully and out again on the other side has been passed using a variety of methods: swimming, wading, *Tyrolean Traverse* and climbing at E 1. *Grade,*' writes Terry Cheek in his Guide.

Having emerged from the East Inlet the Traverse continues into West Inlet or, as we call it, Mother Meldrum's Gut. This dramatic chasm is one of Exmoor's most frightening places. The slope of the east wall offers an escape route up a grassy ridge. The walls of the Gut go parallel, 150 ft, into the coastal slope, with the overhanging back wall towering up to the 120 ft contour. The massive west wall leans out over the floor of the Gut, threatening to topple over on intruders who hang about too long in this dark damp place. This is a world away from Mother Meldrum's Cafe up above, with tourists eating cream teas in bright sunlight.

Above: *Mother Meldrum's seawall Climbers: Philip Osborne & Terry Cheek.*
Left: *Yellow Stone Cave with climbers Adrian Cheek, Clare Tryon, Terry Cheek.*

The seaward end of the west wall is a square-cut vertical cliff, obstructing the Traverse even at low tide. Clemmie Archer waited here in 1958, before swimming out along thirty yards of unyielding seawall to the Yellow Stone Cave. Terry Cheek's Five Day Expedition spent half a night here.

Terry does not like getting his feet wet, so he painstakingly studied the possible moves until he worked out how to climb this wall. The words 'awkward step', 'overhanging corner' and 'descending awkwardly', frequent his description of this VS (Very Severe) thirty-foot climb.

The ledges head on westward round into Yellow Stone Cave. Here the sea has dug out huge blocks of Lynton Beds, to create a rectangular cave reminiscent of ancient temples carved in desert rock. The vertical cliff above the cave has a square face that has attracted dedicated rock-climbers since the 1990s. It is covered in the bright yellow lichens which give it its name.

The Seaward face of Castle Rock

Where the west face of Yellow Stone Headland joins the seawalls of the Valley of Rocks is another cave; a long, thin, slatey tunnel, with a waterfall at the end. The cliffs below the western end of North Walk are less indented and have a broken chaotic texture. The boulders here are unusually green and continue past a single half-tide pyramid, to the wide wave-cut platforms under Castle Rock.

Romantically-inclined observers, walking in the Valley of Rocks, make out a White Lady silhouette, between the rock shapes atop Castle Rock. It is formed by sky seen through spaces in the rocks. The somewhat less romantic boatmen, viewing from the opposite side, and brought up on the TV *Flintstones*, see Barney Rubble's articulated lorry. Geologically speaking however Castle Rock, from inland, looks in the authors' view like a cone, topped with strange rectangular monoliths, whereas from the sea it appears more like a half-cone with an awe-inspiring seaward face, mostly vertical and 300 ft high.

Erosion by the sea has produced this cross-section of Castle Rock, creating a chaotic jumble of stones at every possible angle; in marked contrast to the geometric dignity of the other features already mentioned. Despite the lack of obvious climbing-lines, two Bristol rock-climbers, Ian Parnell and Jim Cheshire, fought a route up the north face of this intimidating cliff, to establish 'Dirty Epic' in 1995.

West of Castle Rock a zigzag path follows the route of a prehistoric waterfall down onto Wringcliffe Beach. On the east side the wave-cut platforms are littered with huge chunks fallen from Castle Rock. The middle of the beach is usually sand and gravel but on the west side it is back to boulders again.

Wringcliffe to Duty Point

The Exmoor Traverse continues westwards across slippery, sea-weedy boulders and past another half-tide pyramid called the Lee Stone. Its summit is a good viewpoint, especially for admiring the aerial grace of the fulmars that nest on the inaccessible parts of the cliffs nearby. More boulders give way to rock terraces below the grassy slopes of Duty Point; a place popular with rod and line fishermen. Suddenly a narrow creek presents a tricky climb. The ledges tend to slope

52

Rocky Tors above Wringapeak Beach

the wrong way, so it is best to get here on a dry day. During 1960 Clemmie Archer and Cecil Agar made two attempts to climb into and out of Duty Creek. They succeeded only at the third attempt, in August 1961. Across the creek, below Jennifer's Tower, are the seaward walls of Duty Point. Good chunky ledges lead around, over deep water, into a little bay of rotten rock, called Jenny's Cove; a classic Lynton Beds rockscape. At half-tide, a seventy-foot wall divides this cove, with a hole through its middle, half-way up. Huge fallen blocks form the foreshore, which then leads on to the low-tide sand of Lee Bay.

Lee Bay to Crock Point

The beach here was once an ideal strand for boats supplying the double limekiln; one of which has been converted into a Chapel by the Lee Abbey Community. The west side of Lee Bay used to be marked by a rock arch, or flying buttress, called Skainer's Hole, which collapsed sometime in the 1930s. By the last bit of Lee Bay sand there is a pair of little caves. The sea comes up to an area of huge boulders again and the foreshore tapers to rising ledges on steep rock. This is the east wall of the low and only flat-topped cliffs of Exmoor. Near Crock Point a vertical *joint-line* fractures the

eighty-foot cliff, from grass right down to sealevel. This is the entrance to a wet tunnel, about a hundred feet long, with several waterfalls in the roof. Having already been soaked exploring this cave, Clemmie Archer tells how he was forced to swim the last few yards to the actual Point.

The dry-shod route around the Point itself is an interesting climb on sheer walls. If one dares to look down there is usually fine surf breaking on big reefs nearby, and a fine view back across Lee Bay to Jennifer's Tower. A high-tide ledge crosses the vertical crack of the cave and then becomes a *hand-traverse* over deep water. The explorer faces two problems here: rounding the Point, a chunk of ledge has fallen into the sea and then there is an eight-foot drop into the gully between the Point and a big rock pyramid.

This pyramid, almost as high as Crock Point, becomes a picturesque island about high tide. Therein lies a story Cyril and Pat Manning used to tell. At the end of one quiet sunny day, sitting out the tide, picnicking and sunbathing on the Point, they left at the ebb and climbed the cliff. Walking back across the grass they met the Fire Brigade coming down: 'Have you seen anyone marooned on a rock cut off by the tide?' Cyril and Pat of course said, 'No' and returned to the car.

As they drove home it dawned on them that some walker or resident at Lee Abbey must have reported them: they had only just escaped being 'rescued'!

Back at beach level the gully leads up onto wave-cut platforms, under vertical cliffs. From a distance the cliff looks solid, with bedding planes dipping to the south at 40°, but the rock is unstable, particularly as it reaches an area of landslip known as Crock Pits: an ancient source of potter's clay.

Coastline showing Foreland Point, Yellow Stone, Duty Point and Crock Point, in the snow of 1991

9. WOODY BAY

Woody Bay and the cliffs of Martinhoe, from the Air

A fine view of Woody Bay may be had from Crock Point cliff top. Directly below is a wide bright beach of reefs and sandy strands, the last sand beach for seven miles. In the foreground, the dark, sheer face of Woody Bay Cliff rises to four hundred feet in places. Here the Hangman sandstones, last seen at Countisbury, re-appear and over-lie the Lynton Beds.

In the middle distance are densely wooded coastal slopes, with a picturesque cottage, limekiln, slipway and fine waterfall at the 'civilised' end of Woody Bay. Way in the far distance the wooded slopes extend north-west, clothing the hog's-back cliff above Wringapeak.

The foreshore, north and west from Woody Bay, is interrupted, firstly by the old pier masonry, and secondly by a little bluff attached by a narrow neck to the main cliff and popular with herring gulls.

Next is a sweep of pebbles, the Manor Beach, which still has the remains of Victorian steps going up amongst the trees. This is a busy and noisy place in the spring, with scores of breeding seabirds on the east-facing ledges.

North of Fulmar's Cove the beach tapers to vertical walls, which become undercut and then overhung, to the point where a tunnel goes right through the neck of Wringapeak.

10. SEA-CLIFFS OF MARTINHOE

uriel Arber, in her 1974 Presidential Address to The Geologists' Association states: 'West of Woody Bay the cliffs rise to a height of 244 m in a hog's-back which continues, broken only by the deep indentation of Hollow Combe, as far as the Valley of Heddon's Mouth' and 'The Exmoor Coast west of Lynmouth runs east-west, parallel to the strike of the beds.' Here the Hangman Sandstones re-appear. The dip-slopes face inland and the *scarp-slopes* face seaward.

The Coast Path climbs up to the 600 ft contour, on hard sandstones, but at beach level the softer *Lynton Shales* predominate. The successive layers of shales have been riven by vertical cracks or *joints*, like saw-cuts; some reach a hundred feet up in the cliff. These joints have been enlarged by groundwater and also widened by wave-attack. The sea has enjoyed carving, sculpting and excavating the shales into a playful variety of stubby headland bluffs and narrow beaches.

Big storm-waves have enjoyed exploding in and out of deep caves at right angles to the shore, and have relished the punching of holes in rock walls to make thru-caves.

Coastal maps indicate how the long finger of Wringapeak Promontary guards the secret world of the Martinhoe Bluffs and Caves. A mile further on, Highveer Point guards the western end of this unfrequented shore.

Of the fourteen bluffs on the hidden edge of Martinhoe parish, twelve have thru-caves, or sea-corridors. These offer a handy short cut for explorers, who want to avoid traversing headlands on wet, wave-worn ledges, above deep swirling seawater. From the corner of Hollowcombe on the Goat Track the tourist can see the well known landmark of Wringapeak with its thru-cave: one of Exmoor's finest views.

Wringapeak

Like the Foreland Point Wringapeak is a convenient place to start a day's expedition along the Exmoor Traverse. There are zigzag paths going down through precipitous woods right out to the headland. Approached on these paths Wringapeak appears as a thin wall, three times higher than it is wide and leaning to the west. A heaven of wild flowers in the spring, the way down is interrupted by a *slump* where an eight-foot drop has gradually appeared since the 1960s. The summit of Wringapeak gives fine views east to the Valley of Rocks and west to Highveer. The headland projects far enough out to sea to give good views of the sheer main cliff, rising to the 500 ft contour, at the stile on the Goat Track. Walkers on the track at Hollowcombe corner looking down on Wringapeak can see a little cairn. It is in fact a stone-wall shelter built by Cyril and Pat Manning, to provide comfort when counting the breeding seabirds on the ledges to left and right. Following tradition we bring stones to the cairn on this crumbling headland. As the tide recedes explorers can descend into a deep gully, opposite a towering *arête*, and down through a boulder *ruckle*, to the beach. The full majesty of Wringapeak and its huge arched tunnel is always impressive. The thru-cave frames a view of Castle Rock, a mile away to the east. At high tide a canoe or rowing boat can pass through with dignity. More boulders lead west to the next headland, Big Bluff, which guards the special place we call The Inner Sanctuary.

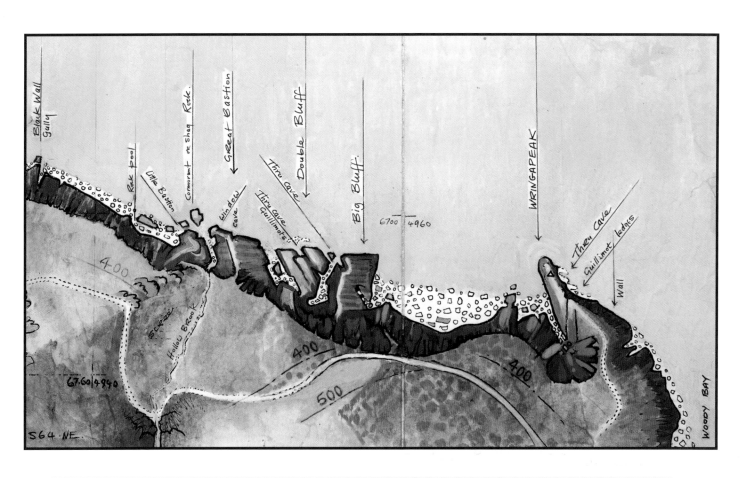

Working Map of Wringapeak showing the Inner Sanctuary, Bluffs and Hollowcombe

Bluffs of the Inner Sanctuary with Hollow Brook Waterfall

Archer and Cecil Agar descended the west side of Hollow Brook waterfall; having already established the route to the beach. At sea level they turned east through a window onto the north face of Great Bastion, the second and biggest of the three bluffs named by the pioneers. Halfway across its face the vertical cliff forced them into the sea, before they could reach the beach of the south-west edge of a twin headland they called 'Double Bluff'.

They scrambled over Double Bluff's fifteen foot high, landward neck and slid down into the dark corridor, under the precipice that had blocked their way westwards from Wringapeak. Close examination of the west wall of Big Bluff showed that much of it was undercut at sea level. The only apparent weaknesses were vertical clefts, one some yards out to sea and another inland, near its junction with the main cliff: nothing offered a way to the east. Rebuffed they turned their backs on Big Bluff to explore, at last, the complex Double Bluff that had eluded them for so long.

Despite failing to get beyond Big Bluff and reach Wringapeak that day, Clemmie and Cecil returned, with some satisfaction, westwards to Hollow Brook.

The Inner Sanctuary

The Inner Sanctuary gained its name because it is the most inaccessible part of the Exmoor Traverse. The main cliff from Wringapeak to Hollowbrook forms a four hundred foot vertical backdrop to a complex formation of rock, with four stubby headlands protruding north into the sea. It took Clemmie Archer two years to complete this section, a distance of only five hundred yards, making five expeditions in all and attacking from both east and west. On the first expedition, in June 1958, Archer followed the Hannington Path, down the Wringapeak Ridge, to the boulder beach and turned west. He examined the first headland, a wedge-shaped feature he named Big Bluff; its flat north face falls vertically into the sea. Archer scrambled up the eastern side to the summit and was delighted with the spectacular view westward over more bluffs, but was dismayed at the yawning chasm at his feet: Big Bluff's west face was a vertical wall of 140 ft! Six weeks later, on a twenty-eight foot tide,

Clemmie Archer spent the next year working on other 'awkward bits' of the Exmoor Traverse, but in the autumn of 1959, he and Agar returned again down Hollow Brook, to make a sentimental pilgrimage to The Inner Sanctuary. They walked down the narrow beach, under the great overhanging wall of Big Bluff, following the tide out further than they had seen it before, and were able to walk dry-shod to the vertical cleft they had seen in July 1958. Archer was astonished to find it was a cave, running fifty yards straight in under Big Bluff.

It was dark inside, and only a yard wide, but suddenly its secret was revealed - two skylights in the roof of the cave! Was this the way from east to west, avoiding the Big Bluff precipice? Realising that they could not climb the smooth, wet walls of the cave, Archer and Agar decided to leave completion of the east to west passage for another expedition.

In August 1960, approaching this time from Wringapeak, they searched the eastern slopes of Big Bluff for the skylights of the secret cave. Sure enough they found a gully full of huge rocks, with two deep holes. The one at the seaward end was five-foot square, dark, slimy and uninviting, but they could hear the sea crashing in the distant entrance of the cave below. They chose to descend by the smaller, two-foot square hole, using a thirty-five foot caving-ladder which happily reached the sandy floor. Then they simply walked out of the cave and stood at the foot of the precipice which they had peered over nearly a year before.

During the 1970s and 80s the Webbs led many such exciting expeditions from Wringapeak, across to Big Bluff and into The Inner Sanctuary. The caving-ladder descent into Archer's Cave and the wade, sometimes a swim out, was always quite an adventure. Terry Cheek, a real 'hardman' but 'frightened of the dark', later established a seaward-route across the vertical north face of Big Bluff, bridging across the cave twelve feet above the water. In 1992, Terry, with Philip Osborne and Clare Tryon put up Way Back, a direct 130 ft climb straight up the west wall of Big Bluff.

Double Bluff

The centre piece of The Inner Sanctuary is Double Bluff. It sits between the two taller bluffs, Big Bluff and Great Bastion, and is a triangular lump of shales, joined to the main cliff by a low narrow neck. The bluff is divided by a vertical fissure widened out at sea level, then tapering upwards to form a tall thin thru-cave. The rock-route Sanctuary which *bridges* up through here was climbed by Terry Cheek, David Hillebrandt and Martine Scholle, in 1995.

In 1959, during their search for the east to west passage, Archer and Agar visited this dilapidated headland of Lynton Shales. They scrambled up over loose slates and piles of rotten rock to the crumbling summit tower, home of scores of young seabirds.

Cyril and Pat Manning visited Double Bluff every spring, especially to count and record the breeding seabirds for the RSPB: the Webb family have continued the tradition. In May and June the whole area of The Inner Sanctuary becomes vibrant with frantic activity: smelling of fishy guano it echoes to the raucous cries of breeding birds. The cave entrance of Double Bluff was once home to nesting kittiwakes and the seaward ledges are still occupied by rows of razorbills and guillemots. The broken slabs of the sunnier landward slope are reserved for a nursery of breeding blackbacks and herring gulls.

Great Bastion

The Exmoor Traverse continues westwards, across a small pebble beach to the east side of the largest bluff, Great Bastion. Rock ledges lead out around, then across the seaward wall of the Bastion. The triangular north face of this very solid bluff, is 200 ft high; its west-facing wall forming the side of Hollow Brook cirque. The ledges end where a finger of rock descends from the main cliff, but a narrow window, nicknamed the 'Yogi Hole', leads through and down safely to Hollow Brook Beach.

Above: *Descending into the Big Bluff Cave. Mollie and Liz squeeze through a boulder ruckle.*

Left: *Mollie ascending Big Bluff Cave via a flexible caving ladder.*

The Vertical Cave that splits the Double Bluff

11. HOLLOW BROOK

In *The Coast Scenery of North Devon*, Newell Arber observes that: 'Between Woody Bay and Heddon's Mouth there is only one feature of interest, the stream known as Hollow Brook. This ends in the highest and finest waterfall of the cliffs of North Devon.' In 1908, Arber had visited Hollow Combe by descending the scree below the Goat Track. He followed the stream to where it plunged over the lip of a hanging valley, but he could not see the waterfall. He wrote to Agnes: 'I have been much worried what to do about the group of hog's-back falls between Porlock and Ilfracombe. Such desperate places to get at I have never seen before and it is absolutely impossible to get to the end of the fall in many places, unless one had a steamboat or a lifeboat; and even then the risk of landing would be great. I am quite sure no human eye has ever yet seen the bottom part of some of these falls ... a great many of them are quite ungetattable [sic] without desperate means.'

Nearly fifty years after Newell Arber's letter, Clemmie Archer visited Hollow Combe in a desperate attempt to enter The Inner Sanctuary. In *Coastal Climbs in North Devon* he describes how, having failed to descend the east side, he and Cecil Agar eventually found a defile on the west side. Belaying 300 ft of cord to a yew tree, they zigzagged down the side of what reminded them of an ice-carved mountain cirque or glacial cwm. They paused to drive in a super-piton and had their first sight of the stream falling 120 ft sheer onto a shelf and then cascading a further 66 ft to the beach; a total drop of 186 feet. They were so enthralled with the view that they dropped a back-pack and 'saw it plunge a hundred feet down the slope in a series of leaps, before pouring out in flight ... one bottle survived intact'. They negotiated steep, crumbling ground, 'deploying ice-axes', and crossed the watery shelf to the east side, where more muddy landslips set them on the beach at the foot of the waterfall. A narrow boulder-strewn canyon took them seaward. At low tide the Hollow Brook stream flows either side of a 30 ft high stack, which Archer called Cormorant Rock. 'In the mouth of Hollow Brook cwm is the broad back of Cormorant Rock. A climb to the top will give a good view of the coast and it is a useful landmark. From the side it looks like a horse's head rearing out of the water' maintains Terry Cheek. From the sea the Webb family think the rock looks more like a pulpit or a lectern, an appropriate photo for the front cover of a book called *The Hidden Edge of Exmoor*.

In the summer of 1968 the 'Brothers Webb' with Peter Hesp and two climbers from Bristol, Alan Tringham and Alan Mitchell, arrived at Town Farm, Martinhoe. Their plan was to follow in the footsteps of Clemmie Archer. They parked their cars between the farm buildings, unloaded their climbing equipment and put on chunky boots. Then old Charlie Ridd appeared. He had a white beard, ten inches long, and walked bent forward with two sticks. 'Wher' be yu off tu, then?' he inquired. 'We're going out to Martinhoe Beacon and down over Hollow Brook waterfall to the beach,' replied the would-be explorers. Old Mr. Ridd poked the bundles of ropes, slings, super-pitons and rock boots with his stick and said, 'Tha' stuff's no oose, they cliffs'll kill 'ee, 'n if t' cliffs don' kill 'ee, t' Gurt fish o' Wringapeak'll get 'ee.' He pointed his other stick at an iron garage with open twin doors and said, 'Tha' fish 'as jaws like they doors ... no'ne 'as ever cum back 'live once t'ey gone o'er t'edge. Tis strit down an' slimey all t'way aside t' waterfall.' 'You seem to know a lot about it,' we said. Archie turned and shuffled off towards his farmhouse. 'O, us oosed t' go down ther' when us wus kids!'

This Hollow Brook waterfall route is particularly spectacular when the stream is in spate, or when it is freezing and the north-east wind swirls the spray around the cirque, draping it in icicles. Despite steep turf, small crags and regular landslips, as well as the Girt Fish of Wringapeak to watch out for, it is an essential access point for the Hidden Edge Traverse. On one occasion, however, in 1991, the Coastguard Inshore Lifeboat, captained by David Taylor, was persuaded to beach at Hollow Brook for a unique photo call. How Newell Arber would have enjoyed such a trip along the coast from Ilfracombe to Hollow Brook, to see the bottom of Exmoor's 'finest waterfall'!

I have been much worried
what to do about the
group of hog's-back falls between
Porlock & Ilfracombe. Such
desperate places to get at I have
never seen before, & it is absolutely
impossible to get to the end
of the fall in many cases, unless
one had a steam boat or lifeboat
& even then the risk of landing
would be great.

Extract from a letter from E.A.Newell Arber to Agnes Robertson (a year
before their marriage), dated Lyndale Hotel, Lynton, 29 August 1908.

" I have been much worried what to do about the group of hog's-back
falls between Porlock and Ilfracombe. Such desperate places to get at
I have never seen before, and it is absolutely impossible to get to
the end of the fall in many cases, unless one had a steam boat or
lifeboat, and even then the risk of landing would be great.
I am quite sure no human eye has ever yet seen the bottom part of
some of these falls.... A great many of them are quite ungettatable
without desperate means."

[I think the reference to a lifeboat (which is inserted) is a result of
his having described a lifeboat display at Lynmouth, earlier in
the letter.

How he would have rejoiced at the way in which you and
your fellow-climbers have now succeeded in seeing these falls!

M.A.A.
23 Sept. 1985]

Hollow Brook Waterfall. Climbers: Martin Blunt & Liz Webb

Hollow Brook Coastguard exercise.
Lifeboat skippered by David Taylor.

12. MARTINHOE BEACON BLUFFS

The 'A' Cave

In 1954, Archer and Agar descended to the beach on the west side of Hollow Combe again: this time they turned left. After five hundred yards of boulders, a smooth slab of black wall and a narrow inlet of sea barred their way. A wade, three foot deep, led onto a stretch of enormous boulders. Then, in his own account, Archer writes:-

'... we came to perhaps the most extraordinary discovery in all our explorations ... a bluff, shaped like a pyramid, with a cave through the east side and a slab of rock, 3 foot thick and 15 feet long, bridging the hole about halfway up ... the pyramid took the shape of a gigantic letter 'A' ... a magnificent bridge of solid rock.'

The two friends climbed up and across the cross-stroke of the 'A' and sat looking westwards along a hundred foot vertical wall. Having decided 'no progress could be made except by swimming,' they then found their way blocked up the seaward stroke of the 'A' by 'hundreds of nesting seabirds'.

Returning to the boulder beach, Archer and Agar climbed the landward stroke of the 'A' to the top of the pyramid and, with no way down to the west, they followed the narrow *col* back to the main cliff, on the east ridge of Red Slide, and then went up to the Goat Track.

The younger generation of climbers, Cyril Manning, the Webb family, Terry Cheek et al., who followed in Archer's footsteps, have been equally impressed with The 'A' Cave. Unlike Archer, they found they were able to proceed westward from this rock-bridge by hand-traversing to a cavernous ledge, then bridging onto narrow ledges to the north-west arm of the pyramid. Wide ledges then lead easily round to a small beach below Red Slide.

The remains of this massive 19th century landslip are still piled against the main cliff, concealing a waterfall that drains the slide. There is just room to squeeze under the huge boulders to view the little fall, No. 18A, if Newell Arber had been able to see it from the boat. The sea is rarely low enough here to gain the next wave-cut platform but a *slit-cave* goes through under the next stubby headland.

The Beacon Bluffs

Red Slide Buttress

The area below Martinhoe Beacon is described by Newell Arber, in *The Coast Scenery of North Devon*, as 'a wild and desolate moorland, ending towards the sea, in extremely elevated and abrupt hog's-back cliffs,' where there is 'a choice of a carriage road high up or a rough path, not altogether safe on a windy day, about halfway down the slope.' At Little Burland Rocks this path, the Goat Track, reaches its highest point at the 600 ft contour. Just east is the long gash of Red Slide. It may have been a fresh red scar when the map makers recorded it for the 1904 Ordnance Map, but it is very green now.

In the summer of 1958 Archer and Agar descended the west ridge of Red Slide, down ever-steepening grass slopes onto Red Slide Buttress. It is just visible from the Goat Track; a little square rock five hundred feet below. From the top of this neat little promontory they could look westward at a 'formidable stretch of cliffs dropping sheer into deep water for 170 yards.' Fixing pitons and cord they climbed down the north-east corner on good rock to the wave-cut platform. Turning east they struggled back to The 'A' Cave, via a deep wade, then returned westward, but apparently failed to notice the thru-cave behind Red Slide Buttress.

The two damp companions arrived on the beach west of the buttress. Strangely again, Archer's Journal fails to mention another cave beside the sheer west wall of the buttress; a huge portal, 15 x 25 ft high and 100 ft deep. With vertical joint-lines soaring up into the main cliff, it forms one of Exmoor's biggest caves; a dramatic scene indeed viewed from a boat, especially when the kittiwakes are in residence.

From this cave there is a one hundred and fifty foot access-route westward up Kittiwake Slab; established by Cyril Manning in 1959. Cyril was a frequent visitor to the seabird colonies in this area and he took Clemmie Archer *en rappel* down the Slab route in 1963.

The 'A' Cave Pyramid (left) with Red Slide Buttress (centre) and the flying buttress

The Flying Buttress

Back in 1958, Archer and Agar pressed on westward into 'the formidable stretch'. 'Vertical faces of bare rock rose for 100 ft with less steep cliff of mixed rock and grass for another 300 ft above that ... Rounding a corner a new feature came into view ... the cliff down into the sea is a grand sweep taking the form of a Flying Buttress. Under it a watery corridor gave access to the next beach.'

Emerging from the corridor Archer and Agar swam, fully clothed, with all their equipment, beneath the overhanging arête of The Claw to a beach ninety yards to the west. They had negotiated three bluffs since Hollow Brook. Each one had involved wading into the sea waist-deep. In later years, Cyril Manning and Terry Cheek established half-tide routes along most of this section, keeping above the beach, and dry-shod.

The Claw

The Claw is a two hundred foot high *pilaster* of rock shelves protruding from the main cliff. During the past three decades it has become an important access route for expeditions descending to the Exmoor Traverse between two of the most difficult obstacles: the east wall of Flying Buttress and the wall that terminates the eastern end of Bloody Beach!

Cyril Manning's Path, down through the heather and entering a steep gully, is still visible from way out to sea. He took Clemmie Archer down The Claw, in 1965, hoping to take him east across to the Flying Buttress, but 'the horizontal traverses on extremely narrow ledges across perpendicular walls' tested Archer's nerve to the limit and he admitted he 'had to funk it'. Between The Claw and the beach is a high-tide platform, above Curate's Corner which terminates Bloody Beach! just west of the caves we call Hannington's.

Red Slide Buttress and Kittiwake Cave (MI)

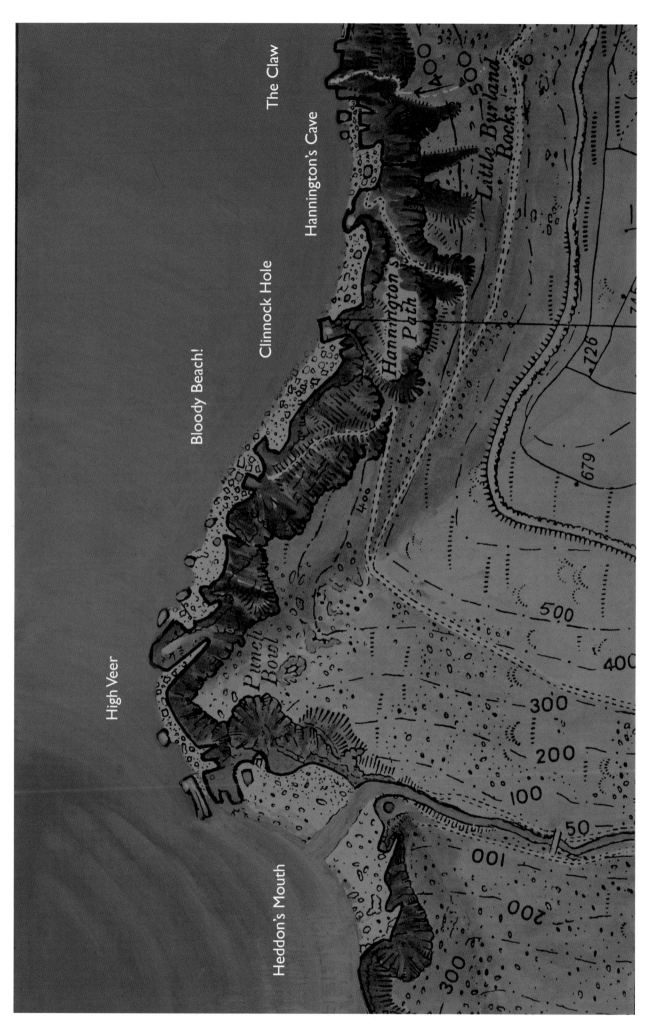

High Veer

Bloody Beach!

Clinnock Hole

Hannington's Cave

The Claw

Heddon's Mouth

Punch Bowl

Hannington's Path

Little Byrland Rocks

13. HANNINGTON'S PATHS

Walkers on the Coast Path, who stop at Little Burland Rocks to picnic or gather whortleberries, have good views westward, along the coastal slopes toward Highveer. They may just notice two faint straight lines in the deep heather, descending diagonally from the Goat Track and disappearing over the cliff at the 400 ft contour.

In 1984 we decided to visit Hannington's Caves via one of his own paths. Of the two marked 'Hannington's' on the 1888 Ordnance Survey Map, Clemmie Archer had used the western path in the late 1950s. He named it the Heather Route. It zigzags downwards under impressive crags, then out onto terrifyingly exposed slopes, with only a string of heather clumps for handholds. We chose to explore the less exposed path, which we consider must have been Hannington's main access route down-over.

It starts well, going straight across and down the heather slope, but suddenly it plunges into a steep gully. This is the course of a little stream, cascading down a rock channel, under some ancient stunted yew trees. A rowan tree belays the five hundred foot of rope required for a safe descent.

Below the trees the gully widens out onto a grassy slope, tilted up at an angle of 50°. The path then descends two hundred and fifty feet in a series of breath-taking zigzags, with apparently nothing between a slip of the foot and the sea far below. All traces of the original path disappear as the grass steepens and gives way to scree and rotten rock.

It must have been at this point, not surprisingly, that James Hannington's helpers, in 1870, began to defect, one by one. When pickaxes dislodged huge blocks of stone to crash and smash themselves to fragments on the beach, and labourer Richard Jones sent a boulder 'whistling down past Hannington's ear', the team spirit evaporated altogether. Only James and George, the Rector's son, were left, with thirty feet to go; every step starting a landslip. Assisted with a rope they descended this 'roguey place', pulling out loose rock as they went. Safely down on the beach, they were delighted by magnificent views of vertical cliffs, the noise of breeding seabirds and most of all by the huge cave, with its three separate entrances. As the boulder beach shrank under the rising tide, they happily climbed six hundred feet back up their amazing path.

Bloody Beach!, below Martinhoe
Photograph by Rev. Oldham in 1897

Hannington's Cave 'Scriven'.

In what we believe is the earliest collection of photographs of Exmoor's remote beaches, a photograph labelled 'Cave Scriven' has been discovered. It was taken by the Rector of Martinhoe, the Revd. R.W. Oldham, in 1897, and shows one of that decade's exceptionally low tides and the distinctive west entrance to the Cave we came to call Hannington's.

The Cave is found deep inside a square buttress, sitting in the corner of the Claw and the main cliff, by Curate's Corner. At high tide the sea floods in through three entrances, thereby gaining depth and increasing the turbulence. Pebbles are carried around in the swirling water, grinding the softer rock strata, enlarging the vertical *joint-fissures,* thumping on the ceiling and generally excavating the whole cavern. The west entrance is beside the main cliff, where a geometric porch-like opening leads into a twenty-foot 'room'. The northern entrances are ten feet lower.

From their sandy floors, perpendicular *mullions* soar twenty-five feet up to the top of the cave. Sea sounds echo and light reflects from the wet walls; creating an impression of an architectural space, characteristic of Exmoor's sea-caves. This hospitable cavern has been the venue of several picnics, even a full-blown barbecue around a bonfire. Such revelry, out of sight of the incoming tide is inadvisable. On one occasion only Terry was sufficiently vigilant to reach the escape platform before the sea flooded in. Seven of us had to swim across to Curate's Corner. Terry agreed to rescue us. We were hauled up the fifteen foot wall, one at a time, to dry out on the Platform in the sunshine, before climbing up the Claw to the Coast Path, six hundred feet above.

According to his diary, 12th January 1871, James Hannington, his college friend Morrell and George Scriven went on an excursion to a cave they called The Eyes. They started from the foot of his cliff path to the eastern end of the boulder beach and climbed the vertical wall to the platform below The Claw. Here they found the slit-cave in the main cliff at high-tide level, squeezed through one of two small holes in the floor and slid down to the lower floor. Hannington then explored another hole and found himself in a large inner chamber with no other outlet. He joked about being caught in there by the rising tide only to find, with horror, that he 'jammed tight' on trying to crawl out. He was forced to strip naked to escape with his life. If they had been unable to climb the smooth wet walls they would have had to wait for the high tide to wash them up onto the platform above!

This little epic was part re-enacted in the 1980s, by Chris Jones and Mike Harris. They descended to the floor of The Eyes, saw the green light through the water and diving through a *sump* they surfaced out to sea, to look back along the vertical walls east of The Claw. They waved to us and then swam back into the cave and happily did not get stuck on the way back. It appears that they did not find Hannington's inner chamber.

Bloody Beach!

Turning west from Hannington's Path, the boulders lead explorers to two small headlands, with thru-caves at half-tide level; one of these tunnels is marked on the map as 'Clinnock Hole'. Although these little caves were interesting, the main attraction for Hannington must have been to visit the impressive cavern he named Cave Scriven.

When Archer descended Hannington's Paths he was intent on passing The Claw; this he did by swimming on ropes to the Flying Buttress and back again. He and Agar then moved further westward, apparently without noticing the three dramatic entrances to Cave Scriven. Passing on through Clinnock Hole and the next tunnel, Clemmie commented that they were wet and 'unremarkable caves and why did Hannington bother!' We can only imagine they were cold and in a hurry against the tide, but the record does show they explored Cave Scriven at a later date. Going west from Clinnock Hole, there are six hundred yards of boulders to cross, with many bigger than cars. Archer found this very exasperating and, as mentioned before, aptly called it Bloody Beach! The beach is terminated by a bluff of Lynton shales, called Highveer.

Reaching the neck of Highveer, the two companions found piles of loose rock slabs and a slippery descent into a gully below Shattered Jack cliff. Further on a small version of Highveer barred their way, forcing them to wade inshore of Ladder Rock Reefs and round onto the beach at Heddon's Mouth. Subsequent Webb expeditions found yet another tall, thin, joint-fissure cave, on the east side of Low Veer, and established the Geoff Moore *chimney-route* to escape the rising tide on Bloody Beach!

Bonfire in Hannington's Cave: Martin Webb, Harriet Bridle and Liz Webb

Martinhoe and Heddon's Mouth from the air

Heddon's Mouth

The Exmoor Coast Traverse may be joined at Heddon's Mouth. The river Heddon is a large stream that has cut a deep valley almost down to sea level. The little cove, with its solitary limekiln, faces north-west, so the Atlantic waves push up a pebble ridge that buries the stream; then, when the river is in spate, it breaks through the ridge again.

In *The Coast Scenery of North Devon* Newell Arber observes, 'The rocks of the shore-line may be examined at Heddon's Mouth, but, in the author's experience, it is not possible to reach the beach at any other point between Woody Bay and Combe Martin, except with the aid of a boat.'

Certainly Heddon's Mouth is the only 'easy' access point and escape route between Woody Bay and Combe Martin, for there are very few places where a boat can go safely ashore. Agnes Arber's diary account of their visit, in September 1910, records: 'We went on again as far as Heddon's Mouth, where we landed. Newell sent the boatman up to Hunter's Inn for a drink, & we had our lunch on the shore.

Then we rowed on a bit to see one or two of the falls. Newell was put ashore in one cove, to examine the waterfall, but there was nothing good enough to photograph.'

Heddon's Mouth was obviously the easiest place for Archer and Agar to begin their first serious expeditions. 'Our advance westward from Heddon's Mouth was begun in April 1955,' wrote Archer, 'with the intention of traversing the one and a half miles to Bosley Gut.'

The way west from Heddon's Mouth Beach soon involves a tricky climb over and across a little half-tide *zawn*. Beyond is a widening rocky beach under rising cliffs below Peter Rock and Philip's Path. The latter was hacked out by Philip Osborne, armed with his own, 'pick-isses, twobills, crowbars and shovels'.

The dark cliffs become more imposing as they build toward Ramsey Head, the north-west corner of Trentishoe Down. Beneath these vertical walls, a wave-cut platform leads around the corner of the headland into the sunlight.

Rough Seas at Heddon Beach with Alan Tringham

Suddenly the explorer is rewarded with one of Exmoor's finest views, a panorama across Elwill Bay to Neck Wood, Holelake and the Mare and Colt, with the magnificent back-drop of Holdstone Down and the Hangman Hills.

At the very point of Ramsey Head, one high, jagged reef continues west, barring the way. A brief exploration reveals where the Atlantic storms have punched a hole through this wall, enabling the Traverse to turn south-west onto the wide, bright beach of Lymcove.

Lymcove

'As the coast of Exmoor runs parallel to the strike of the rock there are few jutting reefs and buttresses comparable to those at Hartland, where the sea is eroding at right angles to the strike of the beds,' observed Muriel Arber in her 1974 Presidential address to the Geologists' Association.

Trentishoe Cove and the Foreland are two such places on Exmoor where the shore-line is at 45° to the general direction of the coast. It cuts across the strike of the rock strata, very reminiscent of Hartland. These places face the Atlantic waves more directly, have wide low-tide beaches, straight tunnel-type caves and big sea-going reefs that sweep down from the cliffs.

In separate expeditions in the 1960s, Archer, Manning and the Webb brothers spent days exploring the gullies, ridges, head-walls and arêtes high above Trentishoe Beach. Twenty years later, Terry Cheek was still following in their footsteps, exploring the Horse-shoe Route, Amphitheatre and Coxcombe Arête. This mile-long beach is easy going, except at the halfway point where the Coxcombe Ridge curves down from the main cliff to form Lymcove Point.

15. LYMCOVE POINT

Five hundred yards north of Trentishoe Church, two bluffs protrude out of the backdrop of Highcliff. The larger twin is Lymcove Point. Both bluffs taper up to knife-edge arêtes. Approached from the Coast Path, the extensive coastal slopes become ridges and gullies at the cliff edge. A steep ridge descends giving a classic Hidden Edge of Exmoor view: to the right huge areas of chaotic cliffs above a rocky foreshore; to the left the orderly upright walls of Highcliff. Across the sea are the island pyramids of the Mare and Colt; then the distinctive blue silhouette of the Hangman Hills. Down below, the ridge tapers to the sharp arête of Lymcove Point, one hundred and fifty feet above the sea. Archer named this The Coxcombe, as the seaward end of the ridge leans over to the north. Terry Cheek is probably the only person to have sat astride this knife edge and inched his way out toward the end. He had to give up and reverse very carefully, when a gust of wind caused a swaying sensation within this pile of shattered Lynton Shale.

Down on the rocky shore, in 1959, approaching from Ramsey Head, Archer and Agar found the north wall of the Point protruded seaward into deep water. They managed to climb up the vertical, fifteen-foot, north-east side and arrived on a narrow platform, where a few steps brought them to a vertical wall dropping down again into the sea. Archer studied this gully with its walls of wave-washed rock and concluded: 'there can be no possibility of ever passing this point without getting very wet'. They clambered down to the south-west extremity of a reef on the seaward side and 'swam for it'. 'It was only four or five yards, but I was well out of my depth,' records Clemmie.

The 'Brothers Webb' and Jeanne Brimson, in 1963, were recognised by Archer as the first to climb dry-shod into and out of this corner gully. This goaded him to reconsider the possibilities and some six months later Clemmie got Cyril Manning to take him across this rock-route. In the 1990s the entire Webb family climbed across the vertical walls dry-shod, but it is still known

to us as The Swim.

Beyond Lymcove Point the beach soon widens again, continuing south-west under the massive Highcliff and ending at the huge gash called Bosley Gut. The weary explorer looks up at an intimidating jumble of fridge-sized jagged rocks that are seemingly poised to fall at the slightest touch. It is an uninviting route, but with the tide at half-flood this is the only way home. The maps of Trentishoe coast show the shoreline going due west from Heddon's Mouth. Rounding Ramsey Head it goes south-west to the corner of Bosley Gut, then turns due west again. This corner is the position of a major fault into the hillside, similar to the fault at the corner of Sillery Sands.

Lymcove Point. 'The Swim' 1964
Peter Ward, Jeanne Brimson, Tim Webb

Looking north up the gentle snow-covered slopes of Hangman, Holdstone and Trentishoe

*The abrupt north face of Trentishoe showing
Ramsey Head, Lymcove Point and the dark shadow of High Cliff*

16. TRENTISHOE BLUFFS

Bosley Gut

Observant walkers on the Coast Path may notice that a gash in the cliff, like Great Red on the Foreland, is creeping inland. Bosley Gut is making for Trentishoe Lane at Southdean Corner; nibbling at the turf and biting chunks off the field on the 700 ft contour! To a mountaineer like Clemmie Archer, this Gut offers a top to bottom passage to the beach. Apart from the hazards of farm rubbish and smelly animal carcasses, the danger of falling objects is ever present. With careless sheep, as well as fellow climbers, kicking off stones to ricochet from up above, a hard-hat is a necessity. Nearing the beach the scree becomes huge boulders, rolled thirty yards out to sea, to form a breakwater and mark the kink in the shoreline. From a boat this gut looks like an open wound in the hillside, reaching right up to the skyline.

Left: *North Cleave Gut with Jon Smith & Clare Tryon.*   Above: *Trentishoe Bluffs and Neck Wood*

North Cleave Gut

From the bottom of Bosley Gut the shoreline turns westward. The beach narrows and the cliffs become unusually indented; like a tall version of The Inner Sanctuary. The Lynton *Shale* rock in the Neck Wood area has been carved into a succession of bluffs, caves with narrow beaches and guts, all reminiscent of Martinhoe's shore. A collection of six bluffs, five little beaches, three caves, five guts and six waterfalls, can be identified along here, below Trentishoe. Rounding the first of the bluffs, emerging from the shadow, the explorer is led into the sunlight streaming down North Cleave Gut.

'North Cleave Gut is a unique sight, even on this magnificent coast, one gets the feeling of walking up the nave of some vast natural cathedral,' wrote Clemmie Archer. Certainly we would agree this gut is one of Newell Arber's 'wonders of cliff-scenery' and a textbook illustration of how vertical joints in the rock allow waterfalls to terminate the evolution of a sea-cave. It is an inlet of the sea that Clemmie Archer describes as '370 ft long, less than 30 ft wide, with parallel rock walls, 250 ft high on the east side and 400 ft high on the west side'.

At the southern end, the back wall has a multi-chute waterfall, about 350 ft high. Terry Cheek and Jon Parkes ascended this watercourse in 2006 and found it 'a very hard scramble'. The low-tide floor is dry right to the shoreline.

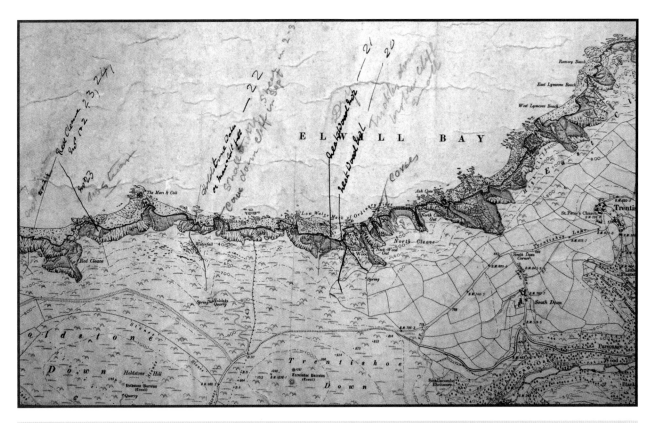

Newell Arber's own annotated map of Trentishoe

There are rock-routes on the west wall of North Cleave, but 'boulder hoppers' can exit left, dry-shod, at the bottom of a spring low tide. Scoured reefs go west to a gut, leading into a most spacious and wonderful cave, certainly deserving of the name Liz gave it: Cathedral Cave. The entrance is guarded by a large iron-rich rock, like a plinth waiting for a carved statue. Passing through a curtain waterfall, thirty feet into the darkness, there is a stone altar waiting for a lighted candle. This is a good place to let go the fears and uncertainties of the present world. A good place to sing: 'You can't kill the Spirit, she is like a Mountain, old and strong she goes on and on and on!' Mother Nature will only ever allow a short moment of reverie before the unmistakable sound of the tide turning echoes in the cave. In a few hours this cave will be under thirty feet of water. So it is quickly off through a tiny 'priest-hole', a convenient escape route which emerges into a shallow parabolic cave, facing west and clearly visible from the Mare and Colt.

From this sunny cave entrance, a narrow beach leads back into the dark main cliff. The next bluff is a curvaceous horned pinnacle, a strange feature with a shallow west-facing cave and its own little beach. The fifth bluff also has a curved pointed summit and a thin beach, below the tallest and thinnest ravine called Neck Wood Gut. Terry Cheek descended the Gut's watercourse from the 650 ft contour in 2009.

Neck Wood

West of Neck Wood Gut, a flat-faced cliff completes the series of six bluffs. Explorers now arrive at Neck Wood Beach; a hospitable picnic spot, good for a paddle. Above the beach is an extensive wooded area, with three ravines; their streams uniting before a final cascade to the beach.

North Devonians, visiting what they call 'Nack 'ude', tell stories of boatbuilders, armed with saws, following down ever-steepening slopes, tying ropes on the trunks of stumpy, contorted oak trees, as they went. Amongst these wind-combed trees, they found ready-curved timber for making the ribs of small boats. The woodcutters probably lowered their harvest to the bottom of the tree line, where they then heaved the branches 'out-over' the last hundred feet onto the beach below. Local boatmen then came ashore, near the Neck Wood waterfall, trimmed the oak branches, loaded up their boats and pushed off for Combe Martin or Lynmouth.

82

One wonders whether the woodcutters returned back up the cliff, or whether they were expert climbers who came in by boat.

Walking along the wide Neck Wood Beach, the last and sixth stream carves a gutter down from a cleft up on the skyline. The exit from the beach is up and over the wall of a long reef, running seaward. The shoreline continues over boulders for three hundred yards, to the boundary of Trentishoe Parish. From now on the Exmoor Traverse is below the sea-cliffs of Combe Martin Parish.

The steep coastal slopes of Hangman, Holdstone and Trentishoe

N eck Wood Beach ends at a sloping headland, its eastern face littered with slabs of broken rock. These are the remnants of Archer's 'favourite route'. Describing the corner of the headland and the main cliff, in *Coastal Climbs in North Devon*, he observes, 'The rocks are formed into a spur of steep, firm *sandstone*, with excellent holds, offering magnificent open views ... we called this the Royal Route. Then a dizzy traverse on steep grass immediately above a gaping void ... and on to the heather slopes above.' Unfortunately this useful route collapsed in the 1980s.

Holelake Cave: West Portal with the Pierced Pyramid. Tim Webb and Jeanne Brimson. 1963

Holelake Cave

Hollowed out of Holelake Headland is Holelake Cave, 'the mother of all caves', a most interesting and favourite place. Approached from the west, it has a lofty, arched cave entrance and a tunnel running eighty-feet east, parallel with the shore. Inside, its boulder floor becomes a little lake (below), some hundred-feet long and twenty-feet wide; perhaps called Holy Lake at one time since it is below Holdstone Down. It is lit by a square window in the north wall, facing out to sea.

This is Holelake's eastern entrance. It is the light, coming from two directions and reflecting the colours of walls, roof and water, that makes Holelake so special. Yet another of the wonders of Exmoor.

Many traversing expeditions, short of time, merely pass through Holelake Cave - in the door and out the window - or vice versa but in 1987, a special expedition was mounted to cross the lake and explore the dark tunnel on the far shore.

An earlier successful attempt to cross water inside a cave, at Whiting Hole in Baggy Point, involved twelve explorers, including the young Webbs and four coastguards. They had first to abseil 130 ft down Scrattling Zawn cliff, carrying cameras, flash guns and torches, before paddling two inflatable boats across the Styx.

Crossing Holy Lake would be a different matter. With the nearest car park at Holdstone Down, 950 ft above, we decided against carrying a boat, but that meant a swim or a wade across dark and intimidating water. Even seasoned explorers seemed reluctant to be first into the mysterious lake. No one was sure what might be lurking in the unknown depths, so everyone swam as fast as possible! The tripod, cameras, matches, rag torches and paraffin were towed carefully, in a plastic bowl on a long string.

Climbing out onto a little beach, the end of the cave turned out to be only a few yards further on. It tapered to head height and contained a little pool full of pebbles; a perfect jacuzzi, rounded out by the continual swirling of water at high tide. The total length of the cavern was found to be one hundred and sixty feet. Journalist Peter Hesp, an authority on Exmoor, joined an expedition to Holelake in 1984. He was so charmed with the place that he gave it the romantic name of the Well at the World's End!

Leaving the underground lake, a dramatic view unfolds from under the curved roof of the west entrance, where a pyramid rock, straight ahead, dominates the intimate half-tide cove. A careful traverse, over lush laver seaweed, leads inland of the pyramid, passing its twin, to end suddenly in amongst car-sized boulders. This is the bottom of an ancient but still active landslip. The Holelake stream carves an ever-steepening canyon in a series of picturesque waterfalls and cascades. Arber's Stream No. 22 finally drops over the lip of the cirque, 120 feet above the landslip. When in spate, or frozen, Holelake Waterfall is visible from Ladder Rocks at Heddon's Mouth.

The stream disappears under the scree and a half-tide inlet leads to a wedge-shaped reef, offering a *layback-climb* up its southern dip-slope. There is no beach here, only the ledges we call Barnacle Traverse; where garden gloves are advisable to avoid lacerated hands. As the reefs taper down to the beach again the Mare and Colt come into view. These two *sea-stacks* are Exmoor's best attempt at making an island!

Beside the pool, Mike Harris and David Taylor steal fire from the Gods

Holelake Waterfall with Martin and Liz Webb, centre

Mare and Colt

The evolution of Hangman Sandstone sea-stacks is demonstrated by the Mare and Colt. Clemmie Archer had a good view of the cliff's 'appallingly shattered and unstable ridge', where more embryonic pyramids can be seen emerging from the ridge to the south; still partially embedded in the cliff and surrounded by scree.

To reach the Mare the explorer needs scrambling and boulder-hopping 'mode'. This pyramid is just short of a hundred feet high. It is formed of sandstone strata tilted up at 40°, with the sea eroding tunnels in the north-west corner. The Colt is about sixty-five feet high and hides a secret: it has a twin, separated by a vertical fissure running due north. The summit of the Colt is an ideal picnic spot, enjoyed by many explorers. The view to the east includes Highveer, Ramsey Head and Trentishoe Down. To the west is an excellent view of Great Hangman's vertical face and beyond that the cone of the Little Hangman and distant Watermouth.

The Mare and Colt from the air at sunset

Red Cleave

From the Colt, a wide open beach curves westward under towering cliffs, to Red Cleave. This large feature is a cirque, with a hanging-valley above a headwall but with a hidden stream; reminiscent of a glacial cwm. At the rim the cliff-climber has to struggle up over a cornice of loose rock and repellent, aggressive heather, to emerge at the 700 ft contour just below the Coast Path. Kester descended Red Cleave one morning with the Sector Coastguard to inspect a wrecked yacht. The Ilfracombe Lifeboats had come to its rescue in the middle of the previous night. With incredible skill the crew of the Inshore Boat, with coxswain Bob Thompson, in shallow water between jagged reefs on an ebb tide, took off the casualties and transferred them to the *Spirit of Derbyshire*, out at sea. Clearly visible were the scars along the rocks where the wreck was dragged by waves. They found the yacht completely scoured out and its contents strewn over the beach.

The Exmoor Traverse continues west but an abrupt headwall, at right angles to the beach, forces a scramble up a ramp to the high-tide mark. Two hundred yards of good ledges eventually give way to a wide sunny beach, stretching away toward Blackstone Point.

Climbers on the Colt watch the approach of the paddle steamer, 'Waverley'

18. SHERRACOMBE (SHERRYCOMBE)

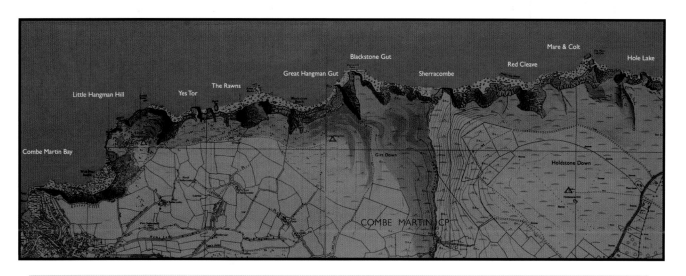

Map of the Combe Martin Parish Shore

Here the Hangman Grits reappear and between Heddon's Mouth and Combe Martin they form the greatest range of all the hog's-back cliffs. The slopes of Trentishoe, Holdstone Down, the Great Hangman and the Little Hangman descend to the sea across the scarp-edges of the beds. The range is interrupted only by the steep entrenchment of Sherracombe (the local pronunciation of Sherrycombe), a valley with sides so steep that it is very difficult of access.' Muriel Arber in *Cliff Profiles of North Devon and Cornwall.*

The Sherracombe Valley was cut by Newell Arber's Stream No. 25, which he observed: 'passes over the rocks in a direction contrary to the dip-slope [creating] a long semi-sheer fall, broken into cascades by ledges of harder rock projecting from the sloping cliff face.'

On 12th September 1910, Agnes Arber's diary records: 'We went on to Sherrycombe where there is a fine waterfall. You could not get far enough away from it on the shore, so Newell was marooned on a convenient rock with the camera and took some photos. Unluckily the sun was shining almost directly into the camera.'

In volume, Sherracombe is the biggest waterfall on Exmoor's coast but only half the height of some waterfalls already mentioned.

An inlet of the sea cuts diagonally south-eastwards terminating the valley, so that the stream falls directly into the sea at high tide. At low tide the stream falls onto attractive pink pebbles. The best view of the fall is on the north-east spur that encloses the inlet. This was once a fisherman's path but the lower part has fallen away now.

During the Second World War German submariners came ashore here, to collect fresh water for their U-boats: a testimony to the remote nature of this stretch of the Exmoor Coast. The steep west side of Sherracombe Valley builds rapidly to form the eastern flank of Great Hangman Hill.

Climbers, Mike Harris, Simon Bell and Philip Draper pause to admire the Sherracombe Waterfall.

Sherracombe Waterfall at high tide, from the air

19. THE SEA CLIFFS OF THE GREAT HANGMAN HILLS

The maps show a great gash in the north face of Great Hangman Hill. This is the largest of all guts with the longest of all the screes. A beach of distinctive, pink Hangman Sandstone boulders fans out to the west of Blackstone Point.

The west wall of the Hangman Gut is the awe-inspiring vertical face of the Great Hangman; described in the Guinness Book of Records as 'England's highest cliff ... the last 700 ft, (213m), of which is sheer.' The craggy head of this face is best viewed from near the top of the Gut, on the old Miners' Track that once serviced five *adits*. Some of the broken, reddish stones in the scree are *deads*, excavated by 19th century iron-miners searching for manganese.

Blackstone Point may be so named because of the occurrence of smooth slabs of manganese ore amongst the pink sandstone pebbles. Above, parallel to the beach, stands the long, high north wall of the Great Hangman. One can see a line of quartz running diagonally, from the adit at the top left of the cliff, down to caves at sea level. A couple of iron spikes show the way up to an inviting 'door' in the cliff face. This is a mining adit which goes in about thirty yards; the home of hibernating horseshoe bats. At the bottom of the quartz band, at beach level, is a sea-cave enlarged by miners to create another adit going in south.

Historic reconstruction, circa 1870, of the Manganese Iron Mines.

Great Hangman: cliff face and scree

The Rawns

The north-east flank of Great Hangman has landslipped from the 720 ft contour, to produce a wide area of active scree known as the *Rawns*.

Agnes Arber's 1910 diary records a boatman's story: 'The women of Combe Martin climbed down the steep cliffs of the Rawns into the cove, & up again carrying as much as half a hundred weight of 'laver' on her back. It takes a woman four or five hours to wash a peck basket of laver, free from all grit etc., & it is then boiled for many hours with salt & vinegar, till it becomes a sort of jelly. The boatman said he liked it very much, & his children would always prefer it to butter on their bread. It grows especially well on a fresh boulder, newly rolled down from the cliff into the sea. He showed us the laver which is like a purple ulva / porphyra.'

It was reported in the 19th century that one woman collecting laver was trapped by the rising tide and drowned on the Rawns. The miners also used a route across the unstable scree; their track still leads from the lip of the landslip back to the col of the Little Hangman. The pinky-mauve stone was mined for iron and manganese ore and also contains fossils of the full-bodied sea-snail, *Naticopsis*. The bivalve *Myalina* has been found above on the cliffs but we have not found it on the beach.

The reddish Hangman sandstone has been popular with masons from Norman times and beyond. The Parish Church in Combe Martin, with its fine tower, has foundations and *quoins* of Hangman stone but local master craftsman, Gerald Walters, calls it 'Rawns'. He records that this stone, freshly fallen from the cliffs in rough blocks, was collected off the Hangman Beaches and brought by boat to Seaside. While it was still 'soft' it was *dressed* and allowed to dry and harden, before being used by masons.

Hangman Stone is also popular with those who get up close and personal with the sea-cliffs. They have found that most of the Exmoor Coast is hard-edged, fine-grained sandstone but further west they find the Hangman stone, with its gritty texture, gives increased friction. They tend to use Newell Arber's term 'Hangman Grits' and have named the north face of Little Hangman Gritstone Wall. Cyril Manning praised Yes Tor for its gritty texture, declaring it to be the finest rock face for climbing anywhere on Exmoor.

The Rawns Landslip and Screes (MVW)

Yes Tor

At sea level below Yes Tor, the beach narrows, passing a narrow foreshore pyramid, aptly called the Shark's Fin. The last bit of beach ends where the vertical east wall of Yes Tor Headland comes out of the main cliff face at a right angle, terminating the boulder beach. The flat north face of Yes Tor is a 300 ft long traverse above the sea.

Clemmie Archer and Cecil Agar had problems with Yes Tor in 1959. In *Coast Climbs in North Devon* Archer writes: 'With some difficulty we made our way through the water across the north face. It was a tide of only 27 ft but the sea was still. We swam for 20 yards and did deep wades for 50 yards over a very uneven bottom that we could not see. During these aquatic operations we scanned the cliff above for a route across but the ledges are too discontinuous. Anyone who ever completes dry-shod the beach traverse past Yes Tor will be a very able rock gymnast indeed.'

Four years later Cyril and Pat Manning established a route across the entire north face, around the north-east corner onto the east wall. Cyril described it as 'the best rock-route anywhere on Exmoor'. Martin Webb, at the age of ten, with his sister, Rebekah, thirteen, completed this traverse section in 1987; illustrating how much easier it is, psychologically as well as physically, for the younger generation to advance on the achievements of the earlier explorers.

North Face of Yes Tor showing use of both High and Low Traverse

After 'aquatic operations' the most hospitable place for Clemmie Archer to 'drain off' would have been on the north-western corner of the Tor, a hook shape on the map. It is a big platform dipping gently south, capable of catching the midsummer sun, and also of providing Terry Cheek with his last campsite during his 1978 five-day expedition. Lying on the seaward edge and peering over reveals nothing but the sea, forty feet below. Route-finding from above, below and from the sides is impossible, because the north wall is so straight and upright.

Little Hangman North Face Gritstone wall from an evening flight

The only way to progress is to climb or abseil down onto the face itself. Here there are narrow ledges of high friction gritstone, tastefully wave-washed into knobs, jugs, deep cracks and chimneys, all with good protection. It is a 'designer' climbing-wall, reminiscent of the granite cliffs of Cornwall.

After a picnic on the sunny slab, the way back to the pub is up Yes Tor Ridge. This arête, overlooking the beach to east and west, is steep, narrow and exposed. It joins the main cliff at a flat working-area, hacked out by manganese miners: the remains of their stone building can still be seen. A track leads east to a slimy gully containing three adits one above the other.

From Yes Tor the beach passes under the sheer Fossil Cliff. A thin, wet gully comes down the corner from the neck of the Little Hangman, filling with red scree as it descends. This is known as Wallover Gut or Yesper Gut.

Terry Cheek and Alan Tringham study the top of the East Face of the Great Hangman. The Great Hangman is recorded as the highest sea cliff in England

20. LITTLE HANGMAN HILL

The Hangman Hills from Watermouth

Now begins a semicircular journey around the robust cone of Little Hangman Hill. The red rock is chunky and gritty, forming a sheer east wall that curves gracefully round to the north-east corner. Two buttresses lie against the wall; the furthest buttress, standing well out, forms a triangular wedge a hundred feet high. This we call The Arête. From here the beach goes west beneath an eighty-five foot high gritstone wall. In 1981, Terry Cheek started putting up graded rock-climbs here; soon to be followed by David Thomas and later, in the 1990s, by Martin Crocker. There were 14 Severe and Extreme graded routes set up from the beach to the grass by 1999.

Easy and rapid progress is possible beneath the face of the Little Hangman, where the wave-cut platforms, parallel with the gritstone wall, are scoured of boulders. As the cliff curves round to the south-west the reefs become submerged, and the fingers of rock point across the bay towards Watermouth. The good gritstone is still on hand

to the left, so a short vertical climb, on big holds, leads easily up to a huge ramp and the arch of the East-West Cave. This cave is parallel to the strike of the rock, tapering inwards for sixty-five feet. The ramp slopes away to the west, with good ledges of reef, leading on and inshore of a high-tide island called the Scotch Stone.

As the foreshore follows around the hill, turning more and more southwards, it emerges from the shadow of the cliffs, out onto bright wave-cut platforms of pinky rock. The cliff itself becomes more indented as it turns across the strike of the beds. Now the reefs extend from the cliffs and gradually get higher, with pleasant southerly dip-slopes.

Rounding the north-west corner of Little Hangman brings the explorer into a shallow cave, facing west. Its huge arched roof collects and echoes to the sound of the waves; the noise heard from the cliff being louder than the sea.

Combe Martin Bay

When the shore turns east-of-south the semicircular journey around Little Hangman Hill is complete. The boulder beach gives way to sand, a luxury not experienced since Crock Pits Beach. This is Wild Pear Beach, known to the old mineworkers, but now with an exit up a tourist path.

Agnes Arber, writing her diary in the King's Arms Hotel, Combe Martin, September 12th, 1910, describes a visit to Combe Martin Parish Church before one of the boat trips she shared with her husband Newell.

'We went out in the morning down to the front, which is not really a "front" but merely the mouth of the two little rivers, one the Umber, which run into the sea practically at the same point. There were two or three boatmen standing about and we asked them if they could take us along the shore towards Heddon's Mouth to see the waterfalls. They said it was quite easy as the weather was smooth & we settled with one of them to start at 11 o'clock.'

'Then we went up again to the hotel to collect the camera, lunch etc., & then having half an hour to spare, we went to see the Church. It is very fine with a great high tower and a perpendicular side chapel. The most striking thing is the beautiful carved wooden screen across the end of the chancel & between the chancel & the Lady Chapel. We went down to the front where the *"Margery"* was waiting for us, & rowed past Wild Pear beach, which the boatman told us is really not "Wild Pear" but "Willper" and on past Little Hangman and Great Hangman . . . We had a heavenly time coming home as we sailed. The weather was perfect, & the sea-cliffs too delicious for anything.'

In the south-west corner of Little Hangman Hill, the sandstone rocks disappear underneath the softer Combe Martin Shales, the *host rock* for silver-lead ore. This corner in the cliffs shelters the hospitable Wild Pear Beach. Leaving this sandy shore, the last lap of the Traverse is across uninviting seaweedy boulders, under the shadow of Lester Cliff. Scrambling over the giant jumble of broken rock, at the shattered neck of the Camel's Head, the explorer emerges at last into the sunlight and civilisation of Combe Martin Beach.

Little Hangman, Wildpear Beach and Lester Point, on the extreme right

The twenty-five mile challenge of the Exmoor Coast Traverse is now complete. From Watermouth Head, looking back east, the Little Hangman stands like the turret of some rococo castle guarding the western end of the Hidden Edge of Exmoor, just as Wringapeak guards the eastern end. We can reflect with satisfaction on a 'proud accomplishment' and know that Newell Arber would have been pleased.

APPENDIX

a. Five-day Exmoor Traverse
Traverse with Three Police Cadets. Terry Cheek

**Day One. Foreland Point: Goat Rock.
6th April 1978.**

We were already in trouble. We needed to take advantage of low water in order to cross the un-climbed area below the Valley of Rocks. But there was a large swell and we were unable to start. Foreland Point has strata leaning to the west, many of the reefs were undercut and flooded on the west side. Once the climbing around the point was behind us, we were able to walk along the beach, with only the problems of Higher and Lower Blackhead Points to slow us down. Cyril Manning was waiting for us at Lynmouth and wished us the best of luck on the next awkward stage.

We had arranged to meet our Communications Group that afternoon, just around the corner at Wringcliffe Bay, where we intended to camp. Having missed the low water under the Valley of Rocks we were forced into serious climbing on an incoming tide. We overcame the flooded East Inlet but came to a halt at Mother Meldrum's Gut, the large West Inlet.

We sat on the ledges above the high water mark for 7 hours and waited for high water to pass. The radio did not work. Because of the need to reduce weight we could not carry water and were relying on streams and springs. It was bitterly cold; we could not sleep or cook. Darkness came and at 10.30 pm we saw the first boulders in the bottom of the gut. We knew that this section to Yellow Stone Cave was just over one rope's length, but it was hard climbing with little protection. We decided to go for it in the dark. With torches clamped between the teeth we made our way across the last 200 ft of cliff at about 30 ft above the water. It took us 4 hours. At 2.30 am we walked into Wringcliffe Bay and woke our Comms Group who were asleep in the boulders. We had been awake for nearly 24 hours.

The following morning we had a conference. Our plans were in shreds. We had climbed for one day and were exhausted. Yes, we had cracked an unclimbed section but we were heavy and moving far too slowly. We were using modern rope-handling techniques with 3 x 150 ft ropes, wet and heavy, and a nightmare to sort out when the four of us were on a cramped ledge. Reluctantly we had to accept that we would have to climb on the low water at night and ditch two of the ropes; one of which we had already left in Yellow Stone Cave. This was later retrieved by Duncan Massey, a local climber who was with the Comms Group. He was also trying to keep our Training Inspector calm.

We had to adopt Cyril Manning's traditional tactics or fail. We devised a system of having the leader and last man climbing conventionally, with belays and runners. The other two made their way along the rope *ferrata* style with two *cow-tails* and had to sort themselves out if they fell.

Day Two:
Wringcliff to Big Bluff

Our plan for the second day was to traverse Duty Point, Crock Point and Woody Bay, through Wringapeak, to the Three Bluffs of the Inner Sanctuary and make Second Camp at the foot of Hollowbrook waterfall, where we would have a supply of water.

We found it difficult on the steep west side of Duty Creek, where the weight of our packs put unbearable strain on the arms and fingers. We made it to Big Bluff, the first of three bluffs without incident. Cyril had told us that we could descend down into a cave that ran through the bluff but we had arrived a little after low water and could not find the entrance. We had failed to reach Hollowbrook Waterfall. Again drinking

Three Police Cadets traversing the Flying Butress below Martinhoe. 1978

water was a problem. We had to collect drips from a spring above to cook the evening meal. We eventually found the cave entrance part way up the cliff, but the sea could be heard 30 ft down in the darkness. There was no way through. We were about 200 metres short of our planned destination, and knew that we would have to make up that distance on the next low water. We settled down in the boulders and slept.

At midnight we dropped into the cave through Big Bluff. We could hear the sea in the darkness but we landed on firm sand. We ran through the length of the cave and to our relief found ourselves on the dry beach between Big Bluff and Double Bluff. This was it! We were committed to 1500 metres of hard traverse with, at that time, only two known escape routes. Luck was with us, we could walk through the cave which divides Double Bluff and along the reef to climb Great Bastion. We had been advised to cross it at about 30 ft but found to our cost the rising strata took us too high. We descended again in the dark to locate the correct line. We passed through The Yogi Hole at the NW corner and immediately heard the roar of Hollow Brook Waterfall, above the noise of the swell. Having already eaten on Big Bluff we settled down for the night. It had taken us less than an hour.

Day Three:
Hollow Brook to Heddon's Mouth

At first light we awoke and from our sleeping bags gazed up at the source of the noise that had been dominating our shallow sleep. It was huge. The volume of water pouring over the top of the cliff was way out of proportion to the small stream that rose a short distance away in Martinhoe. We walked out and climbed the broad back of Cormorant Rock and immediately had a view of the difficulties ahead. The ominous Black Wall totally blocked the route but we were now much further ahead than I had thought possible.

It was now well over a day since we had any contact with the others and knew that they must be concerned for our welfare. But there was nothing we could do, the Coast Path was not in view and the radio required line of sight in order to function. We made it to the foot of the Black Wall, one hour before low water. We climbed the strenuous 40 ft overhanging corner-crack-cum-chimney, on the left side of the wall, at severe grade. We later discovered that this was a first ascent. Easy scrambling brought us to the unmistakable 'A' Cave Pyramid, with its rock bridge joining the main cliff to the Flying Buttress. It was low water now and the sea was calm. We were able to scramble under the bridge and climb onto the wall of the main cliff. We continued west un-roped across the gap of what is now known as Pharaoh's Chimney and down an easy slab to the beach on the east side of Red Slide Buttress. Here we paused, and stared in dismay at its east wall. It was unclimbable.

One of the Cadets wandered into a cave in the back corner of the inlet and came running out shouting that he had found a way through. We passed through easily and came out facing Archer's Corridor Route, under the Flying Buttress. We were in a place where only a few people had ever stood when we heard 'Hello!' from 40 ft above. Nonchalantly perched on a narrow ledge was Cyril Manning, tied on the end of his rope which disappeared up over the grass line. While he was explaining that people were getting anxious, Pete Hopkinson, a Police Instructor, came alongside in an inflatable boat. We bid farewell to Cyril and Pete, informing them that we would camp that night at Heddon's Mouth.

Cyril said he would see us in Combe Martin. He appeared to believe that we were going to make it! We had a quick look around the famous Hannington's Cave and saw Hannington's Path on the slopes above.

The tide had turned. I knew that we had about two hours to get across 650 metres of Bloody Beach! and then we had to climb Highveer Point. We were now two hours into flood tide and the Point presented a strenuous, almost out of reach mantelshelf-move, followed by a climb to the top of Pimple Rock. Once there, it was a gentle stroll down the slope and a reunion with the others on Heddon's Mouth Beach.

It was still cold, as it had been throughout the previous three days. We discussed communications and decided that the radio above us was of no use because of the curve of the hog's-back cliffs. The others went off to Hunter's Inn while we set about cooking a meal and drying out our sleeping bags, damp with condensation. We were extremely tired and not talking much. One of the Cadets who didn't know the route ahead said, 'You know we're going to crack this!'. Quietly I thought, 'Yes it's possible'. We had got further than I thought we would. It was cold, but it was dry and the sea was calm. If it stayed that way we were in with a chance. As I was placing a piton to support the washing line I thought that it could be something small that would defeat us; like a twisted ankle or some other injury. We were vulnerable because we were tired. At this point that I struck my thumb with the peg hammer!

Day Four:
Heddon's Mouth to Little Hangman

At Heddon's Mouth we had a leisurely start to the day. High water that morning was 9.8 metres. We moved quickly, unroped along the tops of the reefs around Ramsey Head and then across Lymcove Beach, and were soon getting our gear on to tackle The Swim. This climb of Lymcove Point went off without incident and we were soon speeding towards Bosley Gut and on to North Cleave Gut. We had been here before and knew what to expect but we were surprised to find that the tide was exceptionally low and we could simply walk into the awesome Gut. By mid afternoon we had passed Neck Wood, boulder hopped to Holelake and on past the Mare and Colt, with only a few rock scrambles before reaching Sherracombe Waterfall. Here we drank heartily.

I had expected this to be our Fourth Camp but the tide was still way out. Was there a chance we could force another 1500 metres to Yes Tor? We decided to go for it. We could always spend the night safely in the bottom of Great Hangman Gut. We passed the bottom of Hangman Gut and out onto Blackstone Beach without climbing. The tide had been coming in for an hour, yet the beach was still clear. I had never seen it so low. Within twenty minutes we were at the east side of Yes Tor: the stepping-stones leading onto the face were still above water. Having traversed Yes Tor, I was getting crazy ideas about finishing the route in Combe Martin that night. But seeing the swell hitting the foot of Little Hangman we decided we had done enough that day and bivouacked on the west side of Yes Tor. The question of availability of water had not crossed our minds when we left Sherracombe Waterfall. Yes, we had made it a little further than planned, but the cost was going to be another cold night without food or drink. We tried the radio and could faintly hear the others calling but they could not hear us.

Day Five:
Yes Tor to Combe Martin

The morning was grim. It was cold and we wanted to end the trip asap. We got moving far too early, the water had not receded far enough. The sea had become angry with white horses visible. We made our way easily across the beach below Little Hangman Gut, but ran into difficulty as we edged along the cliff towards the East-West Cave. The swell was striking the cliff and climbing up towards us. After climbing over The Ramp, and descending to the foot of the Black Chimney, we stood around waiting for the tide to ebb and it began to snow! Balaclavas and hoods over our heads, we stood and stared at the Scotch Stone reef a few yards offshore. Eventually we were able to cross, but our hands were scratched and cut by barnacles, and stung from the wet and cold. Traversing on around the west side of Little Hangman on good rock and boulder hopping from Wild Pear Beach, we arrived at Combe Martin during the morning of the 10th April, 1978.

It had taken us four and a half days. There was no sign of our Comms Group, but the local bobby took a photo. We had stayed on our intended route between the water and the grass line and no one had taken a fall. As far as I know this route has never been repeated in one push, and never done West to East in one go.

NB. I have been asked how it is that the early pioneers took 5 years to complete the Exmoor Traverse yet it only took us less than a week. First we were very lucky with the weather and tide, better equipped, younger and, with the exception of Cyril Manning, much fitter. We used the low water at night so you could argue we took the equivalent time of nine good Spring Tide days. To equal that the old-timers, who only went out on spring tides at weekends, would take nine months, and of course bad weather or lack of a climbing partner would stretch it well beyond a year. We had no route-finding problems, they had already done that time-consuming work for us. They would attack a difficult section from both ends on different days, always turning back when the tide turned, unless they could reach the final point of a previous visit.

They did other things like the exploration of Baggy Point, sketching and mapping, placing stakes for anchors on the escape routes; which also would have to be cleared. Including the planning and recces it actually took us three months. If you include my experience on the Exmoor cliffs over the years and the knowledge gained that was put to use on our trip, there is little difference, between us and the original pioneers, in how much time The Traverse takes. The real reason perhaps is that we really wanted to do it in four days, when the early pioneers would have thought, 'Why?' I have no doubt that if Cyril Manning had wanted, he could have soloed the entire route in two to three days, counting the birds and collecting minerals and fossils as he did so!

I am asked what grade is The Traverse? Cyril would have replied that it varies from 'easy to hard!'. I don't know, we found some VS sections but we had good weather and stayed reasonably low. Weather and tide on the day dictates the line.

Terry Cheek

104

b. Clemmie's Accident, Lymcove

Although Clemmie Archer had completed his Traverse of the Exmoor cliffs by 1960, he still went on establishing and improving access and escape routes in the most remote places. On a damp Sunday, 11th July, 1965, Cecil Agar had lumbago, so Clemmie met Cyril Manning instead at Trentishoe Church. They went up across the field, climbed the stone wall at the 800 ft contour and walked down the coastal slope, following an ever-steepening ridge to the Coxcombe. They tied hand-lines to small rowan and yew trees as they slithered down. In ever-worsening rain, they belayed their rope to a super-piton and descended in the corner of the north side of Lymcove Point and the main cliff. They were controlling their descent, using prusik-loops when Clemmie momentarily relaxed his vigilance: 'I suddenly slipped out of my steps and did what felt like a free fall down 20 ft on to the floor of the gully. I landed on the soles of my feet, but the jar, transmitted up my right leg, fractured my femur'.

Cyril was faced with a well-built, 69-year-old, unable to move at the foot of an 800 ft climb. He followed down quickly and pulled Clemmie above the high-water mark and gave him a thermos of tea. He then began the ascent, rope *prusiking* back up the steep wet gullies and on to the Coast Path. Once there he ran to the farmhouse at Trentishoe to phone for help. The farmer's wife, Mrs. Isaac, was preparing a fifth birthday tea party for her daughter, Angela Spry and her friends.

An hour after the accident the helicopter arrived, but Clemmie was too close in under the cliffs for a direct lift. Meanwhile, first to arrive at Trentishoe Farm from Lynton, was Dr Ernest Mold, straight from his surgery in his smooth, leather-soled, street shoes. He followed Cyril down the steepening cliffs as if it were all part of a GP's day, but admitted later that his service with the Paratroops, during the Second World War, had given him the nerve to 'get on with it!'. He gave Clemmie pethidine while Cyril, for the second time, returned up the cliff.

The Fire Brigade, Coastguard and Police by this time had arrived at the farm and came to the clifftop; followed by Mrs Isaac and all the children from the birthday party. Before Cyril could reach them, the rescue party began to descend with heavy-duty ropes and stretcher, but missing the critical gully they set off down the wrong way. Cyril had to rush down after them to direct them back up and

Clemmie Archer's mountaineering gear

onto the right route. Their rope soon ran out and more lengths had to be borrowed from the other rescue services. With over a thousand foot of rope eventually paid out, the rescuers reached the beach.

For the third time that day Cyril Manning ascended the cliff, guiding the way as Clemmie was hauled up on a stretcher and loaded into the 22 Squadron helicopter waiting in a field at the top. The accident had happened at about 11.00 am but it was an agonising eight hours or more before Clemmie arrived at North Devon Hospital, in Barnstaple. Mrs Isaac's party watched the whole clifftop drama and then went home without their birthday tea!

Dr Ernest Mold and Anne Mold in their picarooner

Although Clemmie recovered from his fracture he never went climbing again. It was his first accident in forty-eight years of climbing. In a detailed account he writes of the accident that 'should never have occurred' and concludes:

'It will be clear that I owe my life, in the first instance, to Cyril Manning, who climbed the whole cliff route twice and the difficult and dangerous lower half a third time - an outstanding feat of endurance and skill in the conditions prevailing at the time. Dr Mold, who is not a climber, also put up an extremely gallant effort; he had a tricky technical job timing the injections to fit the unexpectedly long delays. I have told this melancholy tale, over which I should have liked to have drawn a veil, because I feel there are lessons to be learnt from it which may contribute to the safety of others.'

Clemmie Archer 1965

Dr Ernest Mold's Report;

Compiled from a 1965 account in one of his daughter Anne's climbing books and from a letter to Kester Webb. August 3rd, 2000.

People fall down cliffs and I get a sort of satisfaction over cliff rescues and am used to going down and doing them up. One celebrated occasion was at Ramsey Head, big cliff, something like 600 ft the other side of Heddon's Mouth. I was called out one wet Sunday morning by Cyril Manning who had been climbing with a man named Archer, quite a well-known climber. He had fallen the last 30 ft because rope and piton had given way.

I phoned the police who alerted the ambulance and voluntary fire brigade who were local cliff rescuers. Cyril roped me up and we were well down the cliff when the police arrived. Archer had fractured a femur. Cyril whipped up to organise things at the top while I splinted the femur and gave him pethidine - more suitable and safer than morphia, if injections needed to be repeated.

It was raining hard so I put a coat on the man and made him reasonably comfortable. He chatted away and time went on. I was there three hours giving him a boost of pethidine every hour. I asked what Archer had in his haversack. He said, 'Some beer and some chocolate.' So I said, 'Well, you have the chocolate and I'll have the beer!'

Eventually the fire brigade got down, having had to go back for another 500 ft of rope - 500 ft is usually enough to take with you but it was a tortuous haul. Firemen spaced themselves out down the cliff, each with a crowbar. They drove their crowbars in, the rope laid out along the bars, probably with a half-hitch. The last man lowered a covered rescue stretcher and Cyril and I put Archer on it. I strapped him on (I had already padded and bandaged his legs together).

I attached the stretcher to the rope with a round turn and two half-hitches and signalled to the nearest fireman, who blew his whistle, and the stretcher rose up the cliff as if by magic. I suddenly found myself alone on the beach with a near-vertical mud-slide to climb but I managed to grab an end of the guiding rope attached to the stretcher and hastily put a bowline round my waist!

I got a call-out fee, not very much.

In 1958, Cyril and Pat Manning began recording the numbers of breeding seabird colonies below Martinhoe at Wringapeak, Double Bluff, Red Slide Buttress and Flying Buttress. From the 1970s, the Webb Family went with them on occasion, to learn new skills, and we have continued to visit Wringapeak every May and June since Cyril had to give up. Similar records were gathered by the late Brian Pearce, of the Exmoor National Park, who spied out the birds from his sea-kayak.

The ocean-going guillemots and razorbills that breed here put their knowledge of geology to good use. They know that the best ledges are on the scarp face of the Lynton Shales. Auks do not bother to build a nest, they simply lay their eggs on rock strata that is gently dip-sloping inland. Their cone-shaped eggs have a great variety of background colour, ranging from pale umber to deep turquoise, and a great variety of dark scribbles and blobs all over the shell. Similarly decorated eggs tend to be in the same place every year, so maybe this denotes a family site. Whilst counting the birds on 20th May, 2011, we witnessed a tragedy at Wringapeak when a ledge suddenly gave way and crashed into the sea, taking with it a whole row of guillemots and leaving some dozen eggs exposed for the herring-gulls to feast on. Only three birds returned to their eggs and we assume the others were injured or killed in the fall.

The records over five decades show a decline in most ocean bird numbers. The kittiwakes, with their distinctive cry 'kittiwake', used to nest at four sites, but now only one colony exists, above Red Slide Buttress Cave. Fulmar petrel numbers however have increased; the first record is of a pair breeding at Wringapeak, in 1958. Now there are scores of fulmars nesting all along the Exmoor Coast.

Eggs on a gull's nest

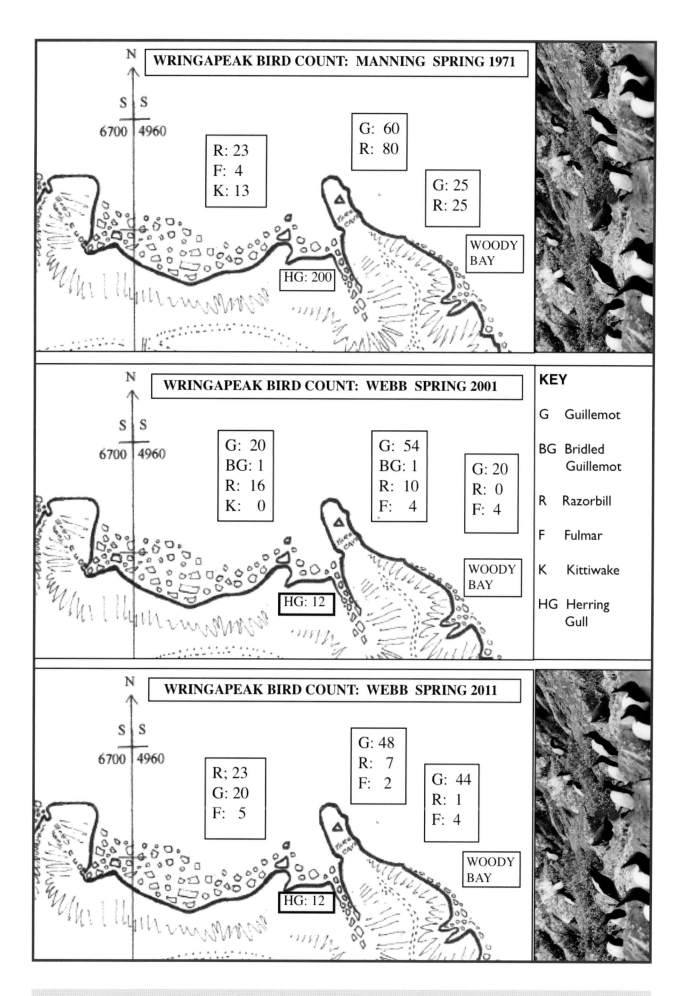

WRINGAPEAK BIRD COUNT: MANNING SPRING 1971

N

S | S
6700 | 4960

R: 23
F: 4
K: 13

G: 60
R: 80

G: 25
R: 25

WOODY BAY

HG: 200

WRINGAPEAK BIRD COUNT: WEBB SPRING 2001

N

S | S
6700 | 4960

G: 20
BG: 1
R: 16
K: 0

G: 54
BG: 1
R: 10
F: 4

G: 20
R: 0
F: 4

WOODY BAY

HG: 12

KEY

G — Guillemot

BG — Bridled Guillemot

R — Razorbill

F — Fulmar

K — Kittiwake

HG — Herring Gull

WRINGAPEAK BIRD COUNT: WEBB SPRING 2011

N

S | S
6700 | 4960

R; 23
G: 20
F: 5

G: 48
R: 7
F: 2

G: 44
R: 1
F: 4

WOODY BAY

HG: 12

Wringapeak Breeding Seabird Count. 1971, 2001, 2011.

d. Seabird Expeditions
Mollie Rodber 1996

Anyone arriving at Woody Bay Car Park one morning in May, 1996, would have sensed something was up by the array of specialist climbing gear set out; including a caving-ladder, watertight containers for photographic equipment, flares and a candle.

We were on one of the Webbs' annual counts of nesting seabirds on the cliff faces between Wringapeak and Hollow Brook. Festooned with ropes we were led off through primroses and stunted old yew trees to scramble down the ridge to Wringapeak shore. A snatched bite of food and we were off westwards and up the rocky incline of Big Bluff, as far as a black hole.

The caving-ladder was being very securely belayed in a corner to hang down into a dark abyss - real adventure now! We descended singly with Liz controlling the safety rope from above and Kester's voice coming up from the void - until a sandy floor was reached thirty-five feet below. Here he had fixed a candle - to give a sort of flickering encouragement! Once landed we crept along this wave-sculpted fissure, a dark, fifty-yard passage. How wonderful then to finally emerge at the special Inner Sanctuary - a very secret and rarely trodden narrow beach.

The breeding season was somewhat delayed that year by the very cold spring but there was much activity amongst the seabirds, with rafts of razorbills and guillemots floating offshore. We carried out the bird count of fulmars, razorbills, guillemots, domineering blackbacks and kittiwakes. With the tide rising we had to return over submerged slippery boulders to the cave entrance and back to climb the ladder.

It was a cause for merriment that I alone became sea-logged to the waist! Never mind, it was a thrilling expedition. With deer trails in all directions, we scaled the cliffs again; where the stalked scurvy grass flourishes and the orpine, first recorded here over a hundred years ago, still grows.

A month later, we again entered the Inner Sanctuary but from its western approach at Hollow Brook; descending two hundred feet beside Exmoor's highest waterfall and passing through a small thru-cave to Great Bastion. Then followed an exhilarating rock-traverse across its face clinging for dear life to the merest fingertip and footholds, with hungry waves just below. We were securely belayed and the whole expedition, as always, had been strategically planned to coincide with the low tide and quiet weather.

This time there was a great coming and going of seabirds, and jostling for space on the crowded slippery ledges; accompanied by a cacophony of guffawing, growling and screeching. The evocative piping of oyster catchers echoed around us. We spotted a few herring gull eggs about to hatch and some very helpless-looking chicks - each huddled under his own rock shelter.

Up on the perilous ledges we saw the blotched and camouflaged eggs of razorbills and the beautiful turquoise-blue eggs of guillemots. Another comprehensive bird-count was taken. The seabird numbers appeared to be slightly down on previous years - but this was yet another wonderful adventure with these intrepid scalers of wild cliffs.

Mollie Rodber

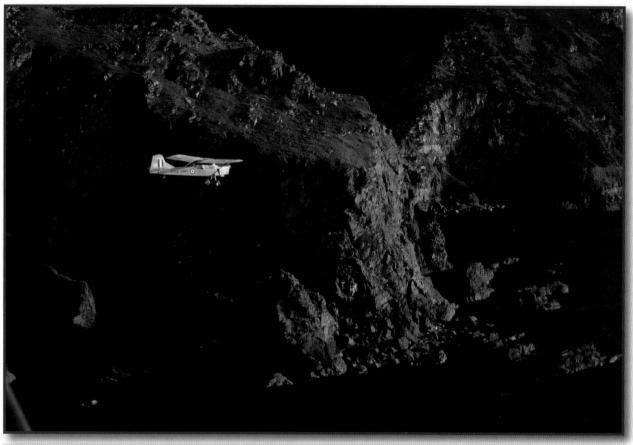

A yellow Auster against the dark seacliffs of Exmoor (BW)

The aerial photographs in this book were made possible by the goodwill, generosity and skill of the pilots who fly us along the coast, low over the sea and often close in under the high sea-cliffs. Their Auster aircraft, built in the 1940s and 1950s for 'air-observation', have been lovingly restored by those who enjoy flying to a mission; such as landing a plane where none has landed before.

A secret fly-in was planned to a remote sandy strand in the six hundred foot shadow of the Hidden Edge. On the chosen day the visibility and the west wind were just right - and the tide duly went out. A dozen ground crew abseiled the cliff, to check the proposed airstrip was firm and clear of flotsam and boulders. We waited at the water's edge, peering up at the skyline of dark cliff-tops.

The sea was quiet, not even a boat out in the Channel, just a few seagulls. The ETA, of twelve noon, came and went. Brian was listening out with the VHF radio but all was silent, only the lapping of waves to be heard.

Suddenly there was an aeroplane a thousand feet up. It was one of ours! It turned downwind and vanished around the headland. Another plane appeared, higher up, then another, and another.

The first plane did a flypast, inspecting the landing strip. We waited nervously as they all disappeared downwind to approach inline. Then around the cliff, thirty feet above the boulders, the first Auster glided in gracefully to make a perfect landing and taxi to the parking area. One after the other the five planes landed safely: one Cub and four Austers.

Mollie on the beach after her first ever flight

Jeff starts an Auster for a quick get-away

The nine aircrew were duly greeted by the smiling ground-crew, and everyone walked around admiring the little planes; the whole extraordinary scene recorded on a dozen cameras. The pilots strolled along this most unusual of landing strips, impressed by the scenery but feeling wary, sandwiched as they were between towering cliffs and the open sea.

The rumour went round that Mollie, at 84 the oldest member of the ground-crew, had never flown in an aeroplane before. She suddenly found herself being loaded into the cockpit of David's Piper Cub and given a VIP flight along the coast she knows so well. Everyone waved as they flew past, the little plane dwarfed by the massive cliffs and on landing she posed with the pilot for photographs.

Kester, on guard duty out on the tide-line, gazing with satisfaction at the five planes parked up, observed that the old Austers, in their wartime camouflage, blended so perfectly with the colours of the coastal terrain, that they were hardly visible from a distance. Suddenly his boots began to fill with sea-water. 'Tide's turned!'

A real life scramble followed as aircrew ran to their planes. There were an anxious few minutes of waiting while propellers were swung to start engines. No 'Plan B'! If an engine refused to fire, the sand, and plane with it, would have been under five feet of water within the hour. But all five planes roared into life and taxied away one by one, accelerating over the ever narrowing strip of sand. Their secret mission accomplished, they lifted up into the west wind and were gone.

The encroaching sea erased the telltale wheelmarks as the ground-crew returned to fixed ropes and happily climbed up the cliff to enjoy a cup of hot tea from Mollie's silver teapot!

f. Photographing the Exmoor Coast

The earliest photographs we have seen of Hannington's Cave and the beach below Martinhoe, dated 1897, shows some dignified-looking ladies in long skirts and a man in a flat cap looking out of Cave Scriven. Maybe they had come down one of Hannington's Paths, arrived by sea or walked along the beach from Heddon's Mouth. Some of the lowest tides ever recorded on the Exmoor Coast were in the 1880s-1890s. Nevertheless it would have been a difficult business for any photographer at that time.

Muriel Arber's Foreword to this book states: 'Much water has certainly flowed to sea, out of Sherracombe since my father, carrying a stand camera and glass plates, landed from a boat to take a time-exposure photograph of the waterfall.'

In *The Coast Scenery of North Devon*, 1911, illustrated with black and white photographs, E.A. Newell Arber expresses his gratitude to his constant companion, Dr D.G. Lillie, for the noble way he shared the labour of dragging that heavy stand camera, boxes of quarter-plate glass negatives and a cumbersome mahogany and brass tripod, as they negotiated steep slopes and screes and traversed rough beaches.

Arber describes the difficulties of photographing on a narrow shore, piled high with great boulders so close to the cliff, as to try the patience of the rising front and the narrow angle lens with its shallow depth of field. The north-facing Exmoor cliffs are 'back-sunneded' so the sun can shine directly on the lens causing intrusive flare effects.

When I first set out to make a photographic record of the twenty-five miles of the Exmoor Coast during the mid 1980s, our camera equipment weighed about a tenth of Arber's timber, brass and glass apparatus.

We also had wide-angle lenses, light metering and 36 exposures of colour film in each little cassette. Even so there were, and still are, plenty of problems for the photographer. Cameras and electronic flashguns need waterproof containers and, with a tripod, add to the bulk and weight of backpacks, already heavy with climbing equipment.

If the climbing becomes severe or the tide is coming in, cameras have to be packed away: so the most desperate and dramatic moments are rarely recorded, unfortunately. Water dripping from above, mist drifting from waterfalls, salt spray rising from breaking waves and the moment when one just has to take to the sea, all add to the difficulties. There was one sad occasion when, unintentionally, I had to re-enact Clemmie's 'Swim' at Lymcove and my classic 'spotmatic' SLR was filled with sea-water.

The wonders of modern photography give us marvellous pictures of the sea-cliffs, but sometimes they still need interpretation. Cast shadows sometimes create ambiguous shapes that can mislead the viewer. In attempting to separate the geology from the biology, the question can arise whether dark bands along the cliff are strata of darker rock, or merely lichen or algae growing at high-water mark. Or again, whether a dark blob is a cave in a rock face, or simply a yew tree.

I use photographs as the basis for topographical drawings and paintings. To expose the underlying geological structures and avoid misinterpretation I illuminate areas of dark shadow and remove vegetation. I also use traditional tricks of the artist's trade, practised by landscape painters, to maximise the visual information and generally enhance the illusion of the third dimension.

Kester Webb

g. A Film for Television 2004

Exmoor Encounters film crew: Jill Radford and Nick Turner, with Kester Webb (MVW)

To celebrate the Fifty Years of the Exmoor National Park, Element Productions of Cardiff made a series of half-hour films for Carlton TV on aspects of Exmoor life. The Webbs' exploration of the Coast was chosen for the first episode: *'Exmoor Encounters: The Hidden Edge'*.

We were first filmed at home in Chelfham where the Film Crew soon put us at ease as we described Clemmie Archer's equipment and showed Newell Arber's photographic glass plates and original prints; returned to North Devon at his daughter's request. Kester was filmed giving one of his slideshows to children at the Pinkworthy Adventure Centre. On the second day, we took the Crew down to the beach at Wringapeak. We fitted the Film Director, Richard Edwards, Sound Man, Nick Turner and Camera, Jill Radford, with hip-harnesses and they fitted us with radio-microphones. Our two hired porters, Terry Cheek and Martin Webb, were loaded with the heavy movie camera, tripod, battery packs and extra ropes. Jill set up her camera at the newly named Radford's Reef, just west of the gaping thru-cave and filmed Martin and Terry climbing the seaward face of Wringapeak.

The next day Liz and Kester descended nine hundred feet down Holelake Stream, to clear vegetation and to belay fixed ropes, in preparation for filming. The following day the Film Crew got safely down the landslip and into Holelake Cave to set up the camera by the lake. Here a bonfire was lit, to add colour to the reflections in the water. We were full of admiration for the stamina and mountaineering prowess of our Film Crew, who really seemed to enjoy the wilderness. Sadly the filming prevented us from attending Muriel Arber's funeral in Cambridge but we hoped to make the broadcast a fitting tribute to her and to her father.

Altogether it was a joyful few days, working with charming, creative people in perfect May sunshine. The results may still be seen periodically on Sky TV but the title 'palæobotanist' is not given to Newell Arber - 'This isn't for BBC 2 you know!' We substituted 'geologist' but in the event the ITV 'voice-over' introduced Newell Arber as someone who came to North Devon because he was 'fascinated by the rocks'!

We think Muriel would be amused.

Kester and Liz with the film crew at Holelake Cove. (MVW)

h. Cautionary Tales of the Hidden Edge

From Porlock Weir to Barnstaple Bay is a watery grave by night and day. This local saying refers specifically to the many shipping wrecks off this dangerous coast but it can also refer to the dangers for landlubbers and trippers, as well as for those attempting to make a living from the sea.

In the 19th and early 20th century four hundred boats a day are said to have plied the Severn Seas, serving the ports of Bristol and Cardiff. Old sepia postcards of Lynmouth Harbour and Combe Martin beach look busy with boats for fishing and leisure trips.

Research geologists have taken advantage of local boatmen to set them ashore along the Hidden Edge. One came down from Bristol University for several summers and relied on local boatman like the late George Eastman to set him ashore and return for him a week later.

North Devon's first research geologist, Newell Arber, with his wife Agnes on a visit to Combe Martin in 1908, hired 'The Margery', one of the rowing boats that went out along the Exmoor Coast as far as Heddon's Mouth; using the flood tide to go out and the ebb tide to get back, with a lug sail in a favourable wind.

The late Ernie Pugsley, one of the last of Combe Martin's boatmen, used to tell how he and his mate, Eddie Lovering, rowed a gig, also called 'The Margery', out beyond the Hangman Hills to Crock Pits. Despite the scarcity of safe places to land they went ashore to collect flotsam and jetsam. They took hessian sacks to collect laver seaweed from the Rawns, rope to bundle up firewood and tow ropes to float big timbers behind the boat.

In April 1940 they went ashore near Ramsey Head and found the body of a Luftwaffe pilot. They loaded him into the gig and took him to the Parish Church where the Rector gave him a Christian burial.

Listeners to BBC Radio 4 *Home Truths* in December 2005 heard how a walking holiday had turned into a nightmare for Alexander Dainty, of Clevedon, Somerset, when he was trapped for two days and a night at sea level on the North Devon Coast. It was clear from his description that he had somehow been lured onto one of the remotest stretches of the Hidden Edge.

Intrigued by his story, and worried his mistake could be made by others, we contacted him through *Home Truths*. It was a relief to discover that the adventure had happened many years ago, before the new, well-signed Coast Path was made.

During the Easter weekend in March 1978, just after leaving Hunter's Inn, Mr Dainty had been 'pixie-led' off the Coast Path and down a sheep track. When it petered out, at the rim of Bosley Gut, he decided to take the tempting 'short cut' that could well have cost him his life. Attracted by the beach, which he judged to be 'fifty feet' below, more like five hundred feet, he slithered down amid a shower of mud and stones and amazingly landed uninjured.

Without a map he had no idea where he was and, having sadly lost his watch on the scree, he had no idea of the time or that the exceptionally low spring tide would mean a correspondingly high tide in a few hours. He set off 'to walk to Ilfracombe'; scrambling and wading in and out of the Trentishoe Bluffs until the rising tide trapped him. He tried to return to Bosley Gut but was forced up under the over-hanging cliffs where he spent the night dozing and waking, hearing voices and having bad dreams.

At the crack of dawn he set off again. He had no food with him but was able to drink from tiny waterfalls. All day he tried to attract the attention of the occasional fishing boat by waving and shouting; he even scratched 'Help' on a rock, not realising he was totally invisible against the dark cliffs. He was in despair and preparing to spend another hungry night on the beach when two lobster potters rescued him off the rocks and took him to Combe Martin.

There a hospitable café owner and one-time 'coachman from Hull' named Mr Fox, fed him and let him have his floor for the night. Next day the boatman went back to rescue his rucksack. A little more research and we discovered that Alexander Dainty had been rescued halfway between Neck Wood and Holelake by George Eastman in *The Star of Scillonia* PW 265. His 12-year-old crewman, Nigel Bird, well remembers the incident.

Our one-time Sector Coastguard, David Taylor, tells of many rescues recorded by Search and Rescue Services, but climbers on the Hidden Edge Traverse rarely come across strangers on the shore. When they do, it is usually to find them driven up the cliff face by the rising tide and unable to get up or down without a rope from above.

In 1960, Kester and Tim Webb rescued an Australian who, unused to such a huge tidal range, thought there had been an earthquake tsunami. In 1980, Cyril Manning, on his way home up the ridge of Yes Tor, spotted a group of four men on the beach by the Shark's Fin. He lowered his rope and hauled them up a hundred feet to safety.

In 2007, Terry Cheek found a man on Blackstone Beach. He had slithered down the side of Great Hangman Gut and had tried and failed to get back up on his own. Eventually and reluctantly he was persuaded that the only way home was to tie on to Terry's climbing rope and accept help. There are no doubt many other such stories that will never be told.

The famous old-time sailor of Lynmouth, Ken Oxonham and his son Matthew, can recall many rescues from Ladywell Beach and Sillery Sands. Several fishermen and tourists were rescued from the rising tide beneath the cliffs of Martinhoe. One day, while out off the Yellow Stone at high tide, Ken saw a man clinging to the vertical cliff, inches above deep water. Ken says, 'I simply plucked him off the rock straight into the boat.'

Terry, are you sure this gorse bush will hold?

Clare Tryon

BIBLIOGRAPHY

Abbot. R. *The Scenery of the North Devon Coast.* 1991.

Arber. E.A.N. *The Coast Scenery of North Devon.* 1911.

Arber. Muriel A. *Cliff Profiles of North Devon and Cornwall.* 1972.
The Cliffs of North Devon. (Geologists' Association Presidential Address). 1974.
The Old Mermaid and other Poems. 1951.
A List of Published Works of Agnes Arber, E.A. Newell Arber & Ethel Sargant. 1968.

Archer. C.H. *Coastal Climbs in North Devon.* (Private) 1961.

Bridle. Harriet. *Woody Bay. 1991. Hannington's Cave* (Exmoor Review 1993).

British Geological Survey. *Minehead District.* 1991.

Cambridge Journals: *E.A.Newell Arber: 1870 - 1918.*

Cheek. T. *Exmoor Walker & Exmoor Climber.* (Websites) 2011.
Climbing Sea-cliffs. (Exmoor Review 1982).

Dawson. E.C. *James Hannington. A History of His Life and Work. 1847-1885.* 1894.

Friend. P. *Muriel Arber:1913-2004.* (The Geological Society of London).

Hesp. P. *Secret Exmoor. Devon Somerset.* 1985.
Exmoor and West Somerset Coastline. (Exmoor Review. 1993).

Keene. P. *Valley of Rocks, Lynton.* Thematic Trails. 1993.

Manning. C. *North Devon* Chapter in Pyatt's *A Climber in the West Country.*

Ordnance Survey Map. 1888 (six-inch).

Pickering. P. *The Geological Foundations of Exmoor.* (Exmoor Review. 1997).

Reason. Joyce. *Bishop Jim: The Story of James Hannington.* London, 1955. 1978.

Riley. H. and Wilson-North. R. *The Field Archæology of Exmoor.* 2001.

Robinson. E. *Muriel Arber:1913-2004.* Geological Society London.

Rodber. Mollie. *An Expedition to Sir Robert's Chair.* (Exmoor Review. 1998).

Webb. D.K. *Climbing Exmoor Sea Cliffs.* (Exmoor Review. 1971).
The Hidden Edge of Exmoor. (Exmoor Review. 2007).

Webb. Elizabeth. *Where are the Books?* Exmoor Society Newsletter. 2007.

GLOSSARY

ABSEIL / ABSEILING: A controlled descent on a belayed rope using a friction brake.

ADIT: A near-horizontal tunnel to mine workings for access or drainage.

ANTICLINE: An arch-fold or upfold in stratified rock. In an anticline the oldest rock will be in the core. The opposite will be a syncline or downfold where the youngest rock is in the core.

ARETE: A sharp ridge of rock between two lower areas. This is usually associated with glaciation, when two glacial cirques may be separated by an arête sharpened by frost action.

BEDDING PLANES: These are planar surfaces which separate one layer (bed) of a sedimentary rock from another. It indicates a break between phases of deposition and such planes can constantly be recognised as shaping many of the surfaces we see in the cliffs of Exmoor, all of which are essentially composed of sedimentary beds.

BEDS / BEDROCK: A bed is the smallest layer or stratum of a stratified sedimentary rock. If it remains solid and relatively unweathered then a mass of beds may be described as bedrock, although the term bedrock is used to describe any solid rock, perhaps underlying superficial or alluvial deposits.

BELAY: A secure point for fixing a climbing rope.

BLUFF: A small stubby headland.

BRIDGE / BRIDGING: Climbing within the gap provided by two close parallel walls (as in chimneying), using equal pressure from hands and feet in opposite directions on the two sides of the gap.

CHIMNEY / CHIMNEY-ROUTE: Climbing using a narrow gap between two, close parallel walls (as in bridging), using equal pressure from hands and feet in opposite directions on the two sides of the gap.

CIRQUE: A French term which has been universally adopted to describe a glacial ice-eroded rock basin with a steep rear wall and steep side walls. It is, these days also more loosely used to describe any deep, upland, armchair-shaped hollow and in that context does not necessarily imply any ice-glacier erosion.

COL: A neck or watershed between two mountains.

COW-TAILS: These are safety cords ending in karabiners, for temporary attachment to safety ropes.

CWM: The Welsh equivalent of a cirque (see above).

DEADS: These are the tailings or waste material from mining operations.

DIP-SLOPE: Geologically, the amount of true dip in a sedimentary rock is the angle of downward inclination of an inclined surface measured at right angles to the strike. In landscape terms, the dip-slope is loosely used to describe a land surface whose gradient is roughly, or approximately, of the same amount and in the same direction as the true dip. As any dip-slope exposure will quickly confirm, an exact correlaton is seldom achieved but it is still a useful general descriptive term.

DRESSED: A stone mason's term for shaping or squaring a block of stone for building.

EN RAPEL: French term for abseil.

EXPOSURE: A geological term to indicate that a bed of rock is exposed at the surface and therefore potentially available for inspection.

FAULT-LINE: Faults result from the rapid release of built-up pressure within the earth's crust producing fractures. In a fault, the fracture in the rock has been accompanied by movement of one side of the fracture with respect to the other. Fractures in a rock that, unlike faults, show no movement on either side of the fracture are simpy known as joints. Its main importance here is that faults and joints provide zones of weakness exploited by weathering and erosion.

FERRATA STYLE: A method of traversing a steep rock route horizontally. There is a fixed steel rope onto which climbers clip a karabiner and slide it along the rope, using cow-tails to transfer past the periodic points where the rope is attached to the rock.

FISSURE: A long narrow crack.

FLYING BUTTRESS: A narrow rock arch extending from the cliff.

GRADED ROCK-CLIMB: Climbs are graded according to difficulty and exposure e.g. D - Difficult; VD - Very Difficult; HVD - Hard Very Difficult; S - Severe; HS - Hard Severe; HVS - Hard Very Severe; E - Extreme. E1, E2 etc.

GRITSTONE: Any coarse-grained sandstone, the grains usually being more angular or sub-angular than in sandstones.

GUT: A narrow channel or cut prior to joining open water. On the Exmoor coast this may cross a wave-cut platform and form a tapering narrow passage into a sea cliff. Its origin may often be traced back to weaknesses in the rocks caused by faults or joint patterns.

HAND-TRAVERSE: Traversing a vertical rock wall using hands and arms without support for the feet.

HANGING VALLEY: A valley whose normal graded long-profile is suddenly truncated, usually by erosion. On the Exmoor coast many local stream courses have been truncated by active coastal erosion. If the valley has an active stream during wet weather then the stream will often leave the valley by a spectacular cascade or waterfall. These coastal hanging valleys are to be distinguished from glacier eroded hanging valleys where large glaciers carve deep valleys truncating smaller less powerful tributary valleys, leaving them perched on the valley sides.

HANGMAN GRITS / HANGMAN SANDSTONE FORMATIONS: The coarse-grained sandstone with some mudstones which dominate much of this Exmoor coast (see map on rear cover).

HOG'S-BACK CLIFF: Hog's-back cliffs, typical of the Exmoor coastline, have developed on the scarp edge of these inland-dipping rocks, the strike of which runs nearly parallel to the coast. The scarp-face supports a seaward slope which is often terminated by a raw, steep, challenging, marine cliff. The photograph on page 100 shows this well.

HOST ROCK: A rock body within which are lodged other, smaller and non-indigenous bodies such as invading veins of minerals. The term country rock also describes the characteristic bedrock of an area, and is again often used in the context of a rock into which an igneous or mineral vein has been intruded.

JOINT/S; JOINTING; JOINT-LINE; JOINT FISSURE: Fractures in a rock which, unlike faults, show no movement on either side of the fracture.

JUMAR: A device for ascending a vertical rope. A metal-handled clamp which slides up the rope and then locks. The clamp tightens when weight is applied and relaxes when the weight is removed. It doesn't move down.

KARABINER or CARABINER: This is an oval metal loop with a sprung or screwed gate. It is used to quickly connect or disconnect to equipment such as ropes.

KARRIMOR SLING: A framed backpack for carrying a child.

KERNMANTLE ROPES: Modern, light-weight ropes for climbing and abseiling.

LAYBACK CLIMB: A strenuous move used when climbing up a slab which has a crack in it by pushing legs in one direction while pulling on the handholds in the other.

LITTORAL: The shore between high and low water levels.

LYNTON BEDS: See Lynton Shales below.

LYNTON SHALES: Variously named in literature as the Lynton Beds and Lynton Slates, the rocks here labelled as Lynton Shales (see rear cover map) encompass an array of different beds which include fine-grained, laminated sandstones, interrupted by thin laminae of fine clays and silts and thin pale limestone fossil-shell beds. The shales are composed of compressed mudstones.

MUDSTONE: A fine-grained sedimentary rock formed from clays or muds. More violent heat or pressure may turn such rocks into shales or slates.

MULLION: A rock formations reminiscent of architectural masonry.

PICAROONER: A small, two-masted fishing boat originally used for herring fishing.

PILASTER: A rock column which projects slightly from a wall, not free-standing.

PRUSIK / PRUSSIKING / PRUSIK-LOOP: A prussic knot is made with a thin rope around a thick rope which can be used as a friction brake for ascending or controlled descending. It slides until it has a load and then it locks. Two are often used, one for your foot and one for your hand, and used alternately.

QUOINS: Cornerstones of dressed stone or brick used for the corners of brick or stone walls to give the appearance of strength.

RAWNS: A local Coombe Martin term for a piece of rock from the Rawn's landslip.

RECCE/S: Slang for reconnaissance.

REEF: An outstanding slab or bed of rock. On the Exmoor coast they are conspicuous when seen running out to sea.

RIB: An upstanding ridge of harder rock.

RIPPLE-MARKED: A fossil sea-bed or sandy shore preserved in rock, showing the agitation due to waves, current or wind which once shaped the sediment before it became rock.

ROCK ROUTE: A recognised route on a rock-face.

RUCKLE: A pile of large boulders blocking a gulley.

SANDSTONE: A rock made from consolidated, rounded sand particles. If the sand particles are angular or sub-angular they are more commonly called gritstones.

SCARP-FACE / SCARP-SLOPE: In general literature, escarpment and scarp have the same meaning i.e. any abrupt slope breaking the continuity of a land surface. However, here, it more specifically relates to the break in slope produced by the exposure of the end-grain of resistant, sedimentary rock beds. In this respect, the coastal slope of the Little Hangman (photo, page 99) provides a good example of the exposure of the scarp-face of the Hangman Grits.

SCREE: An accumulation of fragmented rock waste below a cliff or rock face.

SEA-STACK: An isolated island (at high tide?) of rocks which have resisted marine attack usually by their unusually tough, durable nature.

SHALE/S: A thinly-bedded sediment of clay-grade particles. It splits roughly along bedding planes controlled by the disposition of clay minerals within the rock. In a sequence of fine-grained sedimentary rocks it falls between mudstones and slate.

SLATE/S: A well-laminated, thinly-bedded sediment of clay-grade particles which splits readily into thin plates. This splitting occurs along cleavage planes, planes determined by a history of heat and pressure exerted upon the rock, rather than the planes of the original bedding.

SLIT-CAVE: Weaker beds of sedimentary rock may be differentially eroded to form a narrow cave following that bed through the rock.

SLUMP: The downward slipping of one or several units of rock debris, often with a backward rotation with respect to the slope over which the movement takes place (rotational shearing).

SOLO: Climbing in an exposed situation without a rope.

SPRING TIDE/S: The highest and lowest of extreme tidal range occurring in spring and autumn.

SQUEEZE: A location where access is difficult because of the narrow space between rock faces.

STACK: An isolated rock mass or pinnacle which has been separated from the main mass of rock by erosive processes. This can apply to any detached, steep-sided mass of rock but is most commonly associated with rocks rising precipitously out of the sea (see sea-stack).

STRAND: A beach, sometimes cleared artificially for access by boats.

STRATA: Rock deposits laid down or disposed in layers. Normally, but not exclusively, it refers to beds or bedding of sedimentary rocks.

STRIKE: We generally are quite happy to use strike rather loosely to indicate the general direction of the folded rock structure but more accurately the direction of strike of an inclined surface of rock is a compass bearing of a horizontal line on that surface. It will be at right angles to the true dip of that surface.

STORM BEACH: The mass of coarse sediment, such as pebbles, that collect at the top of a beach marking the maximum extent of deposition by storm waves. The coarseness of a storm beach makes it permeable and therefore less likely to be dragged seawards by the backwash of waves.

SUMP: A length of water-filled passage in rock, like a plumber's u-bend.

SUPER-PITON: A large iron stake used for belaying ropes.

THRU-CAVE: A cave going right through a headland.

TRICOUNI: Alpine style boots with steel nails used for climbing on snow and ice.

TYROLEAN TRAVERSE: Stretching a horizontal rope between two rocks to cross a void either by swinging hand over hand or, if wearing a harness, using a prussic loop.

WAVE-CUT PLATFORM: An erosional surface gently sloping between high and low water. The term implies a platform cut by wave action. However, other shore processes including the constant wetting and drying of rocks, the effect of boring animals, solution and the growth of salt crystals in rock cracks as they dry out. All these help to break up the rock so the term 'shore platform' is sometimes preferred as this is purely descriptive and does not imply that it was formed by one process.

ZAWN: A steep-sided inlet in cliffs, usually the product of differential erosion by the sea. It is a term in common use in Cornwall and the south-west. The name is sometimes used where the inland end of a coastal cave has collapsed exposing a 'yawning' hole in the roof of the cave similar in some ways to a blowhole.

DAVID KESTER WEBB

Kester Webb was born and bred on the Brendon Hills, within the Exmoor National Park. At the age of 15, he won a major scholarship to study at Somerset College of Art, later specialising in Landscape Painting. He went on to graduate in Art Education and Special Education from the Universities of Cardiff and Exeter, respectively.

He and his wife, Elizabeth, came to live in North Devon in 1971. He taught pottery, craft and outdoor activities at Lampard Special School in Barnstaple, until his retirement in 1995. Kester has spent a life-time exploring and making a photographic record of the remote coastal region of the Hidden Edge of Exmoor, giving talks throughout the West Country. This book marks the culmination of his, and his family's, experience of exploring and recording this remarkable and unique stretch of coast.

ELIZABETH WEBB

Liz Webb would say that her training to participate in the Exmoor Traverse began on the hockey fields of the Lincolnshire Wolds, where she was born and spent her early childhood. Her love of gymnastics and the outdoors continued at University where she obtained a 1st class BA Hons degree in Theology with History whilst at the same time playing for the All English Universities (WIVAB) hockey team.

A career in education followed, taking a series of teaching posts in higher education. Whilst studying for her Master's Degree at Bristol University and looking for something different she joined a pottery class run by a Kester Webb, who introduced her to the wonders of the Hidden Edge of Exmoor.

After they moved to North Devon, Liz took a post lecturing in Religious Studies at North Devon College and serving as an Open University Counsellor in Humanities for North Devon. A post she 'immensely enjoyed' until 2000, when she joined Kester in retirement.

Left: *The North Walk along the seaward face of the Valley of Rocks.*
A bird's eye view in the light of dawn.

Looking west through Wringapeake Cave with Yew Trees on cliff slope in the background.

Looking east through Wringapeak Cave across Woody Bay to the Valley of Rocks

North Devon Thematic Trails

Thematic Trails is a not-for-profit educational publishing charity specialising in publishing literature which, through education as a source of pleasure and recreation, aims to increase our understanding, interpretation and appreciation of valued environments. Our **North Devon publications** are as follows:

The Hidden Edge of Exmoor
David Kester Webb and Elizabeth Webb (2011) ISBN 978-0-948444-57-9

Classic Landforms of the North Devon Coast
Peter Keene (1986,1996) ISBN 978-0-948444-58-6.

Lyn in Flood, Watersmeet to Lynmouth
Peter Keene and Derek Elsom (1990, 2003) ISBN 978-0-948444-20-7

Valley of Rocks, Lynton
Peter Keene and Brian Pearce (1993, 2000) ISBN 978-0948444-25-8

The Cliffs of Saunton
Peter Keene and Chris Cornford (1995) ISBN 978-0-948444-24-1

Braunton Burrows Ecology Trail
Janet Keene (1996, 2003) ISBN 978-0-948444-30-2

Exploring Barnstaple
John Bradbeer (1990, 2002) ISBN 978-0-948444-42-5

Exploring Bideford
Peter Christie (1989, 2000) ISBN 978-0948444-31-9

Northam Burrows Estuary Environments
Janet and Peter Keene (1997) ISBN 978-0-948444-33-3

Westward Ho! Against the Sea
Peter Keene (1986, 1997) ISBN 978-0948444-34-0

The Cliffs of Westward Ho! a sense of time
Peter Keene (2004) ISBN 978-0948444-35-7

Bucks Mills, people and place
John Bradbeer (2011) ISBN 978-0-948444-56-2.

The Cliffs of Hartland Quay
Peter Keene (1989. 2006) ISBN 978-0-948444-46-3.

Geology at Hartland Quay
Alan Childs and Chris Cornford (1989) ISBN 978-0-948444-12-8

Strawberry Water to Marsland Mouth
Peter Keene (1990) ISBN 978-0-948444-06-7

This selection of North Devon walks, guides and landscape companions, published by Thematic Trails, may be bought at information centres, museums and shops local to sites, or may be obtained directly from Thematic Trails by contacting us at the address below. A fully illustrated catalogue of 250-odd publications stocked by Thematic Trails, together with further details of this literature can be inspected by visiting our web site: **www.thematic-trails.org** which also has purchase facilities on-line or by post.

Thematic Trails

7 Norwood Avenue, Kingston Bagpuize, Oxfordshire, OX13 5AD
For advice or information:
Telephone: 01865 820522   or   Email: keene@thematic-trails.org
Thematic Trails is a not-for-profit registered charity no 801188